Tony Rossiter

Effective
Negotiations

In easy steps is an imprint of In Easy Steps Limited
16 Hamilton Terrace · Holly Walk · Leamington Spa
Warwickshire · United Kingdom · CV32 4LY
www.ineasysteps.com

Notice of Liability
Every effort has been made to ensure that this book contains accurate
and current information. However, In Easy Steps Limited and the
author shall not be liable for any loss or damage suffered by readers
as a result of any information contained herein.

Trademarks
All trademarks are acknowledged as belonging to their respective
companies.

In Easy Steps Limited supports The Forest Stewardship Council (FSC),
the leading international forest certification organisation. All our titles
that are printed on Greenpeace approved FSC certified paper carry the
FSC logo.

MIX
Paper from
responsible sources
FSC® C020837

Printed and bound in the United Kingdom

ISBN 978-1-84078-593-7

1 Why negotiate

We negotiate instinctively every day of our lives. We can't always have everything we want. So we have to give and take – in other words, to negotiate. And whether we're discussing a family outing or negotiating a major IT contract for our company, the best outcome is likely to be a win/win agreement that everyone can live with.

Introduction

"To confer with others in order to reach a compromise or agreement." That's the dictionary definition of negotiation. It's something we do every day, like it or not. It doesn't have to involve contracts or business deals. It might just mean agreeing a deadline for the task you're doing, sorting out office space or talking to your boss about your vacation plans.

We can't always have our own way. Sometimes we have to settle for less than we would ideally like. We have to give and take – in other words, to negotiate.

Whether we know it or not, we're all negotiators – even children. In some ways children are better negotiators than adults. They use any means they have to get what they want:

- A baby screams when it's hungry or it needs a clean diaper

- A child soon learns that eating up every last bit of broccoli will get them the ice cream they really want

- A teenager may bargain a clean and tidy room against permission to go to a late-night party.

Parents use the same negotiating techniques. "Can I have some chocolate?" asks the child, and the parent responds: "If you clear all your toys away, I'll think about it."

Negotiating is something we do instinctively every day of our lives – with our family, with shopkeepers and sales people, and in the workplace.

Some books assume that negotiation is all about buying and selling. Of course, if you're buying or selling something you'll want to get the best deal you can. That goes without saying. But buying and selling is not the be-all and end-all of negotiation. Far from it: there are many other scenarios.

Beware

We all negotiate instinctively every day of our lives.

Negotiating scenarios

Partner or family

If you have a partner or a family, chances are that you won't always agree about everything. And usually it's not the big things in life – things like religion or politics – that cause most conflict. Often it's the little things. Those are the things we tend to argue about – things like:

- Which TV program shall we watch?

- Shall we take the children to the park or the beach?

- Which restaurant shall we go to?

- Which route shall we take?

- Which brand of coffee shall we buy?

However close we are to those around us, we often want something slightly different. That's life. Most of these things are pretty unimportant and the little decisions we have to take don't matter very much; most of these are everyday, run-of-the-mill decisions, taken on the hoof. Probably the decision will not be given much thought. It may depend on the personality of the people involved or the mood they happen to be in or how strongly they feel about it. If you're not too bothered, you might simply accept what someone else suggests. You might just want a quiet life.

If, on the other hand, if you do feel strongly about it, you'll want to argue the toss and to suggest something that suits you better. You might not get exactly what you want; but you might well be able to avoid something you would really hate. By negotiating (even if you don't call it that or even recognize it as that) you'll have come up with something that you can both live with.

Friends and neighbors

Outside the home, too, there are many situations and circumstances in which negotiation skills come in useful. For example, you might find yourself negotiating with neighbors about babysitting, or looking after the dog or cat while you're away, or sharing responsibility for the school run, or keeping an eye on your house while you're on vacation.

Beware

A negotiation is not a battle.

Hot tip

Look to build a long-term relationship with the other side.

...cont'd

Companies and customers

If you're buying a new car, you'll want to get the best deal you can. You'll probably haggle over the price; over what's included in the deal. There are lots of things that can be thrown into the melting pot, like the delivery date, method of payment, the color and a hundred and one extras that you may or may not need. Then you'll have to take out insurance, and you may be able to haggle over the premium and the terms and conditions. You can negotiate different deals with different energy suppliers, telephone companies and internet service providers. Some will say: "This is what we can give you: take it or leave it." Others may be prepared to negotiate on some aspects of the deal.

Buying or selling an apartment or a house is a common negotiating scenario. If you're buying, you'll probably want to offer less than the asking price. If you're selling, you'll need to be clear about the minimum you will accept. Both buyer and seller will need to take account not only of their own personal circumstances and priorities, but also of external factors such as interest rates, the state of the housing market and so on.

If you work in sales or purchasing you'll probably be involved in discussions with customers or clients or agents about prices, delivery dates, commission rates, product specifications, transportation, servicing and so on.

Professional contacts

Depending on the type of work you do, you might find yourself involved in discussions and negotiations with professional contacts such as lawyers, accountants, academics, etc.

Colleagues at work

There are lots of situations – some relatively straightforward and unimportant, others complex and critically important – where decisions need to be taken and you have to reconcile what you want with what your colleagues or your organization are prepared to give. These discussions are not always called "negotiations", but very often, in order to arrive at a solution which everyone can accept, you have to settle for less than you would ideally like. You need to give and take – in other words, to negotiate. Common examples include:

- Budget allocations

- Job roles and responsibilities

- Pay and working conditions

- Office accommodation

- IT equipment

- Work priorities, objectives and targets

- Demarcation disputes

- Vacation plans

...cont'd

Contractors

These days most organizations contract out a whole range of support services – things like:

- Office cleaning

- Travel

- Transport

- IT support

- Training

- Security

- Catering

Someone has to negotiate all those contracts.

Government agencies

There's often scope for arguing about the interpretation and implementation of laws and regulations on such things as planning, taxation, health and safety, company law, and so on. You could find yourself discussing stuff like this with government agencies, regulatory bodies and others.

Internal stakeholders

For any important negotiation you'll almost certainly need to have some internal discussions first. You'll need to get all the key people on board and signed up to your negotiating objectives. These discussions will probably include senior colleagues in your department or in other parts of the organization and other key internal or external stakeholders who are affected.

These internal negotiations are sometimes the most difficult of all. When I worked at the Department of Trade and Industry and represented UK interests at EU negotiations in Brussels, the preliminary discussions between different Whitehall departments, thrashing out an agreed UK negotiating position, were sometimes more difficult than the subsequent negotiations in Brussels.

There are many different negotiating scenarios. The good news is that the principles and techniques of effective negotiating apply to all of them.

The need for compromise

Compromise is not a dirty word. On the contrary: it's the name of the game. Negotiation implies compromise. The key objective – always – is to reach an outcome that is acceptable to both parties. A good negotiation is not a battle. It's a contest, with each side trying to get the best deal it can of course – but not at all cost.

Shafting the opposition is unlikely to be a good idea. You'll almost certainly have to deal with them in the future. So it makes sense to ensure that the other party also gets something out of the negotiation. That way, you have a much better chance of building a long-term, mutually beneficial relationship. Sometimes maintaining a good long-term relationship is even more important than the outcome of a single negotiation.

So it makes sense to make sure you understand where the other side are coming from, and to show concern for their objectives. The aim should be a win/win outcome. Whatever the context (except, perhaps, buying a second-hand car from a salesman you'll never see again), it's always sensible to think long-term. If you pull a fast one on someone today, they may do the same to you tomorrow. If the outcome of a negotiation is a clear win/lose and the losing party feels that they have been taken advantage of, they are likely to remember this for a long time. That's human nature. It's only natural for the losing party to resolve to get their own back next time.

Negotiation means compromise.

Summary

- We negotiate instinctively every day of our lives

- Negotiation is not just about buying and selling

- By negotiating you might not get everything you want, but you might well avoid something you'd really hate

- You can negotiate with family, friends, neighbors, companies, customers, clients, professional contacts, work colleagues, contractors, government agencies, internal stakeholders

- The same principles and techniques apply to all negotiating scenarios

- Often in order to arrive at a solution everyone can accept, you have to give and take – i.e. to negotiate

- Preparatory discussions with internal stakeholders can sometimes be more difficult than the negotiation you're preparing for

- Negotiation means compromise

- Look to build a long-term relationship with the other side

- If you pull a fast one today, the other side may do the same to you tomorrow

- Aim for an outcome that's acceptable to both sides

- A good negotiation is a contest, not a battle

2 Key principles

These key principles apply to every conceivable negotiating scenario. Whether you are having a family discussion about next year's vacation, talking to your boss about your need for a new laptop, or negotiating a multi-million dollar contract for your company, these are the foundations that will enable you to achieve a positive result.

Key principles

Here are the three keys to effective negotiation:

1 Clear objectives

2 Thorough preparation

3 Good personal relationships

Put these foundations in place, and you'll have an excellent chance of developing the skills and techniques needed for effective negotiating. We'll be looking at each of these in more detail later. This chapter gives an overview.

Clear objectives

The first principle of any negotiation is to be crystal clear about your objectives.

What is it that you want to get out of it?
Sounds pretty obvious, doesn't it? Plain common sense, but if:

Start out with clear objectives.

- you've been preoccupied with other, perhaps more urgent, tasks, or

- it's a subject you're not very familiar with, or

- it's a complex subject raising lots of issues which you have not yet been able to get your head round, or

- you're pressed for time,

then it's all too easy to arrive at a meeting with only a very fuzzy idea of what you want to get out of it. And that's a recipe for disaster.

Of course, it's possible that you'll have to modify your objectives as the negotiations proceed. That happens. In fact, it's not at all unusual. There might be some new development which you – and the others around the table – need to take into account. Some new facts might emerge that affect the negotiations. These might strengthen your arguments and put you in a stronger position. Or the other side might come up with facts or arguments that weaken your position and make it unsustainable. In either case, you may well need to modify the objectives you set yourself at the outset. But it's imperative to begin with a very clear idea about what you want to achieve.

We'll look at objective-setting in more detail in Chapter 4.

Make sure your facts and figures are 100% accurate.

It's often hard information that wins the day.

Thorough preparation

The better prepared you are, the greater your chances of success. It's as simple as that. Preparation means:

- Mastering the facts and figures: making sure you have all the relevant stuff at your fingertips. In any negotiation it's usually hard information, not subtle argument, that wins the day.

- Checking for accuracy: making sure that the factual information you're going to use is 100% accurate. If it isn't, this will seriously damage your credibility and weaken your negotiating position. So check and double-check for accuracy.

- Consulting colleagues, experts or specialists who know more about the subject than you do.

- Rehearsing the presentation of your case.

- Finding out as much as you can about the positions, objectives and underlying interests and concerns of the other side.

- Finding out as much as you can about the people you'll be negotiating with.

We'll look at all this in more detail in Chapter 5.

Good personal relationships

Good personal relationships are often the difference between success and failure. Most of us find it easier to talk to, and to deal with, people we know. So take the time and trouble to get to know those you'll be negotiating with. It's worthwhile putting a great deal of effort into this. It can be the most important single factor in achieving a successful result.

If you can establish some kind of personal rapport with the people around the table, chances are, you'll feel more relaxed and this will make it much easier for you to get your points across. It will also help to promote the kind of friendly, constructive atmosphere in which any negotiation is most likely to succeed.

If there's an impasse and things get really difficult, a close personal relationship between the key people can make all the difference in the world.

Good personal relationships can be the key to success.

Summary

- The three keys to effective negotiation are:

  – clear objectives

  – thorough preparation

  – good personal relationships with the other side

- It's essential to start out with crystal-clear objectives

- Be prepared to modify your objectives as the negotiations proceed

- Preparation means mastering the key facts and figures and checking for accuracy

- Usually it's hard information, not subtle arguments, that wins the day

- Consult experienced colleagues or other experts

- Rehearse the presentation of your case

- Find out as much as you can about the other side's objectives

- Get to know the people you'll be negotiating with

- A close personal relationship between the key negotiators is often the key to success

3 Core skills

Negotiation does not require any skills that are unusual or difficult to acquire. Most of the core skills involved are likely to be within the competence of any effective manager. As you gain more experience of negotiation they can be developed and enhanced.

Core skills

Here are the principal skills you'll need for effective negotiating:

- **Oral expression:** the ability to express yourself clearly, concisely and convincingly

- **Logical argument:** the ability to construct an argument based on logic and order, rather than emotion or personal opinion

- **Analysis:** the ability to identify and get to grips with the key facts and to examine arguments critically

- **Listening and questioning:** key skills – not as easy as you might suppose – which can be developed and improved with practice

- **Prioritizing:** the ability to rank your objectives and to view them in the context of your organization's wider priorities

- **Interpersonal skills:** the ability to relate effectively to others – arguably the single most important attribute of an effective negotiator

Let's look at each of these in a little more detail.

Oral expression

To negotiate effectively you need to present your case clearly and concisely – and with conviction. That means using the kind of skills you would use if you were making a presentation or taking part in a meeting. Speak clearly and succinctly – with energy and conviction – and not too fast. You need to make an impact. So don't waffle.

Remember that a negotiation is not a debate. Don't try to score points off the other side. If there's a problem you need to address, do not question the other side's intentions or motivations. Instead of criticizing what the other side did or said, make them understand how you feel about the problem and focus on explaining it in terms of its impact on you or your organization.

If it becomes clear that the other side see things differently, recognize this explicitly. You can acknowledge that the two sides are faced with a joint problem, and propose and encourage a joint approach to finding a solution.

Logical argument

Practice how to argue a case logically.

Your ability to argue a case logically can be improved with practice. Take an issue – any issue you like – on which there are two clearly opposing points of view. Prepare a logical argument to support one of these. This should be a logical process, with one point following another as you build up the argument, together with supporting information and examples to prove your point. Write yourself a brief speaking note. Then find someone who supports the alternative point of view. Argue your case as convincingly as you can, but try to come to an agreement.

Then turn it on its head – prepare a logical argument, complete with supporting information and examples, to support the alternative point of view. Again, try this out on someone who disagrees, and try to come to some kind of agreement.

A politician who's preparing for a TV debate or an interview usually practices by getting a staff member to play the role of the opponent or interviewer, with instructions to give him as hard a time as he can. Politicians are adept at arguing a case, regardless of their personal beliefs. If you practice in the same way you will develop the ability to present an argument based on logic, rather than emotion or personal beliefs.

Try to develop a line of logic to support each point you make. Wherever possible, use specific examples to illustrate your points.

Analysis

Analytical skills are important because you'll need to put the other side's case under the microscope. You'll have to look very critically at their proposals, checking their facts, figures and technical details for accuracy. You'll have to examine their statements and consider whether their conclusions are logical and whether they are based on evidence. You'll have to decide whether their arguments really stand up. The better prepared you are – the more familiar you are with the factual background to the negotiation and the more you know about the other side – the easier all this is.

Listening and questioning

Sometimes we hear what we want to hear – not what is actually said.

Listening can be hard work. It's easy to hear what someone is saying without really taking it in. We all do it every day, when someone is saying something we're not really interested in. We automatically switch off. We just pretend to listen.

Good listening skills are crucially important. All too often, we hear what we want to hear, not what is actually said. It's essential to concentrate throughout the negotiation. Absorbing information and getting to grips with the key points requires a conscious effort, and that's not always easy, especially if the discussion has gone on for most of the day and the speaker is less than riveting. It's very easy to let your attention wander, to think about the novel you're reading or the holiday you're planning. Don't succumb to that temptation.

Long, impenetrable sentences might contain vital information or hidden clues. The uninteresting manner of speaking might even be a deliberate ploy to conceal or skate over weaknesses. So pay close attention to what is said. Concentrate on every single word. Look at whoever is speaking and fix your attention one hundred percent on what (s)he is saying. It might be boring, but it's what you're being paid to do. And it might enable you to pick up vital information or clues that you can use to support your own case or to counter the arguments of the other side.

Active listening means showing that you are really interested in what's being said – even if you're not. You can do this by looking at the speaker and making eye contact, occasionally nodding your head to indicate agreement or raising your eyes to show that you're puzzled or unconvinced, and taking notes of key points.

Use questions to get to grips with what they're saying.

Questions are your main tools in cutting through the verbiage and getting to grips with what the other side are really saying; understanding the facts and assessing their arguments. They can also be a useful way of cooling things down if the discussion becomes heated. If there's an emotional outburst, or you are attacked aggressively or personally, resist the temptation to respond in kind. Don't question the other side's motives or their integrity. Just wait patiently until they have got it off their chests. Then either stay silent or respond calmly with rational questioning. Rather than defending your position, use questions to put the ball in the other side's court and to show that you want to be positive and to move forward. Focus on the future. Ask questions such as:

- What would you suggest?

- How can we deal with that?

- What alternatives are there?

- What kind of solution do you envisage?

- What adjustments do you have in mind?

In Chapter 8 we'll look at how listening and questioning skills can be put into practice. Together with critical analysis, these are the main tools you'll use when you scrutinize the other side's case.

Learn to listen actively.

27

Prioritizing

It's essential to prioritize your aims and objectives. Some will be more important than others. Separate needs from wants: things you must have from things you'd like to have. We'll be looking in more detail at how objectives can be set and prioritized in Chapter 4.

A negotiator also needs to have a clear understanding of the wider priorities of his or her organization. How does this particular negotiation fit with:

● your own work targets,

● your department's financial objectives,

● your organization's corporate strategy, and

● the wider importance of maintaining a good relationship with the other side?

Interpersonal skills

Interpersonal skills are at the heart of effective negotiation. You need them both during formal negotiating sessions and, even more importantly, during informal discussions.

Networking can make all the difference. The more people you know, and the better you know them, the greater your chances of success.

When I worked at the UK's Department of Trade and Industry I was involved over a period of six years in many EU negotiations in Brussels. The longer I was doing the job, the more I realized the value of informal contacts and quiet, one-to-one discussions. Sometimes these took place in the corner of the meeting room, but more often it was over a coffee or a beer or over lunch in the canteen.

When negotiations became really difficult and there were huge differences of approach, these differences were rarely settled in the conference room. More often informal, often bilateral, discussions resulted in greater understanding on both sides and a consequential softening of positions, eventually enabling the deadlock to be broken.

In Chapter 6 we'll look in more detail at how you can use your interpersonal skills to build a strong personal relationship with your opposite number(s).

Networking can make all the difference.

Summary

- Core negotiating skills are:
  - oral expression
  - logical argument
  - analysis
  - listening and questioning
  - prioritizing
  - relating effectively to other people

- Speak clearly, concisely, with energy and conviction, and not too fast

- Practice building up a logical argument, supported by hard facts and specific examples

- Check the other side's facts and figures for accuracy

- Examine the other side's statements and arguments very critically

- Listening is of prime importance

- Concentrate on every word and don't let your attention wander

- Listen actively and show the speaker that you are listening

- Use questions to get a clear understanding of what the other side are saying

- Prioritize aims and objectives and separate needs for wants

- Interpersonal skills are at the heart of effective negotiation

- Informal one-to-one discussions can help to break a deadlock

4 Objective-setting

Setting clear objectives is the first essential for any negotiation. This chapter gives some common-sense, straightforward guidance on how you can go about setting objectives and incorporating these into your negotiating position.

Make sure your
objectives are SMART.

Be SMART

Your negotiating objectives should be:

- Specific

- Measurable

- Achievable

- Relevant

- Time-limited

S pecific
M easurable
A chievable
R elevant
T ime-based

Specific: the more detailed and precise your objectives, the better.
Avoid generalities and imprecise or ambiguous words and phrases.

Measurable: you need to know whether or not your objectives
have been achieved, either in full or partially. That means setting
objectives which can be measured. Figures or values, such as
quantity or cost, are often the best way of doing this.

Achievable: It's a waste of time setting objectives which are never
going to be achieved. You have to recognize reality. Objectives
should be challenging, but achievable.

Relevant: the objectives need to be fit-for-purpose: relevant to the outcome you are seeking to achieve.

Time-limited: deadlines help to concentrate the mind. Establish the timescale within which you will aim to achieve your objective(s).

In anything other than the simplest negotiation, you're likely to have several objectives, and you'll need to reach agreement on a number of different elements. Some will be more important to you than others. So it's essential to prioritize. Begin by identifying the must-haves. Then go on to add additional objectives you believe you have a good chance of achieving. The last category consists of those things you might achieve in an ideal world – if absolutely everything goes your way. So your objectives can be divided into:

- those you must have

- those you'd like to have, and

- the icing on the cake

You can incorporate these into a hierarchy of negotiating positions, as:

- Ideal outcome

- Fall-back position

- Bottom line

- BATNA – best alternative to a negotiated agreement

Ideal outcome

This is what you would hope to achieve in an ideal world. Chances are, you won't get it. You're unlikely to achieve absolutely everything you're seeking. But just occasionally, if everything goes right for you and all your arguments are accepted, you might get close to it – for example if, for one reason or another:

- You're in a really strong negotiating position, and

- The other side are keen to reach a quick agreement

Your ideal outcome needs to be really ambitious – something that's going to be really difficult to achieve; something which, in all likelihood, won't be achieved. But don't go totally over the top. There's no point in having an ideal outcome which you know for certain is never, ever going to be achieved.

Fall-back position

Your fall-back position should be an outcome which you could live with and which you believe has a realistic chance of being acceptable to the other parties to the negotiation. There may be precedents which will provide clues as to what is likely to be acceptable. You'll almost certainly need to carry out research or do some detective work. The more you know about the positions, interests and objectives of the other parties, the easier it will be for you to judge what they are likely to be able to accept. Your fall-back position needs to take account of the interests of the other parties. But it also needs to be something which, though not ideal, is perfectly satisfactory to you.

Your fall-back position needs to be acceptable both to you and to the other side.

Bottom line

Your bottom line is the absolute minimum that you can accept. It's important to work this out before you sit down to negotiate. This is the line in the sand beyond which you will not go, whatever concessions are offered or whatever pleas or threats are made. This is the point at which you refuse to be party to any agreement.

If you do get pushed to your bottom line, it's always worth asking for one further concession from the other side.

During the six years that I represented the UK at one of the Council Working Groups that meet in Brussels to hammer out differences between members of the European Union, I was involved in lots and lots of negotiations. Only on one occasion did I get close to achieving the ideal outcome. Usually, the result was somewhere between the fall-back position and the bottom line – and it was often closer to the bottom line.

Best alternative to a negotiated agreement (BATNA)

The final – and critically important – piece of the objective-setting jigsaw is to work out the pros and cons of not reaching an agreement. No agreement is usually better than a bad agreement. You need to be quite sure that your bottom line is more attractive than the alternative of having no agreement.

Your negotiating power relative to the other party or parties depends upon how attractive the alternative of having no agreement is. If your BATNA is very attractive, it's sensible to spell out to the others why you would be quite content for no agreement to be reached. If, on the other hand, your BATNA is pretty unattractive, it makes sense to keep it to yourself.

An important part of your preparation (see next chapter) should be to find out as much as you can about the options of the other side in the event of there being no agreement. If both sides have attractive BATNAs, the best outcome for both may be no agreement.

Beware

No agreement is better than a bad agreement.

Summary

- Set objectives that are:
  - specific
  - measurable
  - achievable
  - relevant
  - time-limited

- Avoid generalities and ambiguities

- Prioritize your objectives

- Divide objectives into those you must achieve, those you'd like to achieve, and those you might achieve in an ideal world

- Work out a fall-back position that's acceptable to you and has a realistic chance of being acceptable to the other side

- Work out a bottom line that's the minimum you can accept, and make sure it's better than the alternative of having no agreement

- If you get pushed to your bottom line, ask for one final concession before you sign up to an agreement

- Remember that no agreement is better than a bad agreement

- If both sides have attractive alternatives (BATNAs), no agreement may be the best outcome

5 Preparation

The better prepared you are for a negotiation, the greater your chances of success. It's as simple as that. Preparation consists of a number of elements. It includes having an in-depth understanding of your own case and, so far as possible, of that of the other side; learning lessons from previous negotiations; and thinking not only about your negotiating aims and objectives, but also about the concessions you're going to make.

Understanding yourself and the other side

The Chinese military general and philosopher Sun Tzu (544-496 BC) wrote:

"If you know your enemy and you know yourself, you need not fear the result of a hundred battles. If you know yourself but not your enemy, for every victory gained you will also suffer a defeat. If you know neither the enemy nor yourself, you will succumb in every battle."

Sun Tzu was a military strategist and he was talking about war. It's a mistake to treat the other side in a negotiation as the enemy. A win/win outcome is invariably better than win/lose. Nevertheless, what Sun Tzu had to say about preparing for war is equally applicable to preparations for a negotiation. It's vital to have a full understanding both of yourself and of the other side. You need to know what each side has got that the other side wants.

Don't forget

Failure to prepare is one of the commonest reasons for unsuccessful negotiations.

Failure to prepare is one of the commonest reasons for unsuccessful negotiations.

Learning the ropes

If you're new to negotiating, don't jump into an important negotiation right away. Take it steadily, in easy steps:

1 Do some preparatory reading. There is no shortage of literature about the principles and practice of negotiation. This book is a good starting point.

2 Find out as much as you can about previous negotiations similar to those you're going to be involved with. Study some relevant case histories. This might mean digging out old papers or talking to colleagues who were involved.

3 Get your boss or an experienced colleague who is conducting a negotiation to take you along as an observer. Your role will be to watch, to listen and to learn.

4 Then go along as an assistant. Try to agree beforehand exactly what your responsibilities will be. These might involve presenting facts and figures to back up your negotiating position or handling one small element of the negotiation.

5 Take personal responsibility for handling a negotiation that's not too important.

6 Once you have been through the above steps you'll be ready to handle an important negotiation yourself. The first time you do this, make sure you have some back-up: either someone alongside you during the negotiation or an experienced colleague close by whom you can consult if you need to.

Learn to combine firmness with flexibility.

Rehearsing

Whether you're negotiating on your own or as part of a team, it's always worthwhile rehearsing. However thoroughly you prepare on paper, it's not the same as performing for real in an actual negotiation.

Ministers in the UK routinely prepare for sessions in the House of Commons by getting an adviser or an official to simulate the questions he or she might have to face from Members of Parliament. One Minister I worked for would always say "give me as hard a time as you can."

One of the best ways to rehearse is to role-play: get a colleague who is an experienced negotiator to play the role of the other side. Remember that you are not role-playing yourself; you are doing it for real, doing the job you're paid to do – trying your hardest to achieve a good (win/win) result.

A variant of this is to persuade a more experienced colleague to role-play your part. You can watch and see how they would handle the negotiation. You'll be able to see what works and what doesn't. You can learn from seeing how brilliantly (or how badly!) they perform.

If it's an important negotiation, you'll need to prepare by having a full dress rehearsal, using real data and rehearsing your statements and arguments. Get someone to take notes of the rehearsal so that you can review it afterwards to see what improvements you can make.

Learn from previous negotiations

Look at how previous negotiations with the same party went. Re-examine old minutes and notes and talk to colleagues who were involved. Find out how the other side behaved. How did they operate? What was their strategy?

But remember that things may be different now. Some of the key factors may have changed. What was important and relevant last year may now be less important or less relevant. Or there may be some developments, which were not important or relevant last time, which you now need to take into account.

Once you've had some experience, think about what you have learned. Review some recent negotiations, and consider to what extent your objectives were achieved. If you achieved a good result, try to identify the reasons. If the result was not very satisfactory, think about what you could have done differently. Think about how you presented your case and what kind of relationship you had with those on the other side of the table. However successful you were, there's always room for improvement.

Learn from previous negotiations.

Team roles

If you're negotiating as part of a team, it's imperative to agree beforehand exactly who will do what. Everyone must be fully briefed. It's essential for all members of the team to be mutually supportive and to sing from the same hymn-sheet. Contradictory messages will undermine the team's credibility.

In a three-person team, it's usual for:

1   **The team leader** – and only the team leader – to make proposals and respond to the other side's proposals

2   **A second team member** to act as technical expert, providing detailed facts and figures as necessary and responding to the other's side's requests for factual or technical information

3   **The third team member** to act as note-taker, keeping a careful record, in particular, of key offers and statements made by the other side

In a team of five (usually the largest number for an effective negotiating team), the above roles are sometimes augmented by the addition of:

4   **The good guy:** someone who expresses sympathy and understanding for the other side's point of view

5   **The bad guy:** someone who opposes the other side's point of view and seeks to expose their weaknesses and undermine their arguments

Of course it's possible for the above roles to be combined and for the same person to play more than one role – or to play different roles at different stages of the negotiation.

But for any important negotiation, a team of two really is the bare minimum. Two heads are always better than one. You can agree in advance who will handle what, and bounce ideas off one another about how you'll handle things. During the negotiation one of you can watch, listen, take notes and – importantly – think, while the other one speaks. If one of you flags, the other can take up the cudgels. And while one of you is speaking the other can be marshaling his or her thoughts. The combined efforts of an effective two-person team are always greater than the sum of its two individual components.

Sometimes you'll have to negotiate on your own. That's not ideal, because a negotiation can be a pressurized environment and one person operating alone can feel the strain. It's not easy to listen to what the other side are saying, think about your response and take notes – all at the same time. But if you're in sales, negotiating with prospective customers, that's likely to be the norm. That can be tough, but the more you do it, the easier it will get. Thorough preparation is the key.

Your own case

Look at the process of preparing your case as a three-tiered pyramid:

THE
OBJECTIVE
FACTS AND
FIGURES
THE FOUNDATION

1 **At the top is the objective** – what you are seeking to achieve. This includes the ideal outcome, the fall-back position and the bottom line, together with the BATNA.

2 **Next, supporting the objective**, comes the hard information – the key facts and figures that underpin your negotiating position.

3 **Finally, we have the foundation** – the underlying interests and concerns on which the whole edifice is based. These may include factors such as: profitability; interests of, or pressure from, key stakeholders; the organization's strategic aims and objectives; wider economic, financial or political factors; long-term relationships.

Having a clear understanding of your organization's underlying interests and concerns and, critically, of how these may be affected by the outcome of your negotiation, will enable you to see the negotiation in a wider context. If the negotiation has a number of different elements, this may help you to decide how much weight to give to each element. Or it may be that the maintenance of good relations with the party or parties you're negotiating with is more important than the outcome of this particular negotiation.

Do your homework. It's vitally important to have a thorough understanding of the subject-matter. Take the time to brief yourself thoroughly. Look at all the relevant papers. Talk to colleagues who've been involved in the past. You might need to consult experts or specialists who know more about the subject than you do. Make sure you have the key facts and figures at your fingertips. Get them into your head. You'll probably want to take some notes into the negotiating room with you, but it's better if you don't have to rely on them.

Prepare yourself as you would prepare for an exam. Go over the key information again and again until it is lodged firmly inside your brain. Then you'll be able to tap into it spontaneously as the need arises, either during the negotiating session or when you're chatting to fellow negotiators informally. Showing that you're in total command of the subject-matter – that you can readily call up the key facts and figures – will earn respect and enhance your credibility.

It's vital to cover every angle and to ensure there are no key omissions. If there are any gaps in your information base which the other side can identify and exploit, it could seriously undermine your negotiating position. Gather together all the facts and figures you may conceivably need. It's better to have too much information than too little. If the other side ask a straightforward factual question which you can't answer it, it could be embarrassing and could undermine your credibility – especially if the question is one you could and should have anticipated.

It's as important to analyze your own position as it is to find out all you can about the other side's. Identify your strengths and weaknesses. Think about how you can make the most of your strengths, and assemble the key:

- Facts

- Statistics

- Precedents

- Arguments

- Specific examples and case studies

Make sure you have the key facts and figures at your fingertips.

47

...cont'd

Look for any potential weaknesses in your case and think about how you can deal with these. It's a good idea to put yourself in the other side's shoes. If you were in their position:

- What objections would you raise?

- What questions would you ask?

- What aspects of your case would you home in on?

- What changes would you seek?

Make a list of the objections, questions and changes you have identified. Then think hard about how you can respond. Make sure that for each point the other side are likely to make, you have the ammunition to deal with it – facts, figures and arguments.

Now think carefully about how you can make best use of all this information – how you can present your case clearly, concisely and effectively. Write yourself a brief speaking note. You won't want to read from a script. That will give the other side the impression that you lack confidence or don't know your stuff as well as you should. It will also make it impossible for you to make eye contact with the other side – and that's very important. But a brief speaking note – perhaps just essential facts and figures and a few key words to serve as memory-joggers to remind you of arguments, examples or anecdotes – is a useful prompt to keep you on track and ensure you don't forget anything that's vital.

The other side

Preparing for a negotiation does not only mean getting your own house in order. It's vital to think about the other side. You need to find out as much as you possibly can about them before you sit down to negotiate. Think like a detective! Gather as much in-depth information as you can about:

- **The people you'll be negotiating with:** their backgrounds, experience, roles and responsibilities, specific concerns and so on. Talk to people who know them.

- **The organization you'll be negotiating with:** find out as much as you can about their strategic aims, financial performance, sales figures, production and marketing successes and failures, etc. Trawl all available sources: company accounts, annual reports, Chairman's speeches, mission statements, press releases, publicity and marketing material, etc. Use the internet and libraries to carry out market research and track down relevant trade journals and press cuttings.

Don't skimp on your research. It should help you to understand where the other side are coming from. Again, try to construct a three-tiered pyramid:

1 **Their objectives:** previous negotiations or agreements may give you some indication of their likely objectives. As with your own objectives, try to prioritize and to decide whether these are likely to be regarded as essential or merely desirable. Pay particular attention to the importance they're likely to attach to reaching an agreement – and to how they would view a failure to agree. In other words, have a stab at working out what their best alternative to no agreement (BATNA) would be.

2 **Facts and figures supporting their objectives:** some of the facts and figures underpinning the other side's negotiating objectives will probably be the same as yours. But there will also be some related specifically to their own organization, and some of these may well be in the public domain. So find out as much hard information about them as you can.

...cont'd

 Their underlying interests and concerns: identifying these – the key influences that have played a major part in determining their negotiating objectives and positions – is often the most difficult part of the pyramid. Some of these may be pretty obvious or may become apparent with a little probing, but others may be closely guarded secrets, especially if they provide evidence either that they:

● are desperately keen to reach an agreement, or

● attach very little importance to reaching an agreement

The more you know about the other side, the better. And the better you know the individuals you'll be negotiating with, the easier it is to ascertain not only their likely negotiating objectives but also the interests, influences and concerns which drive them. Identifying and dealing with those interests and concerns is often the key to success. And the key to identifying those is often a close personal relationship with the person or people you're negotiating with. Use informal social events and business networks to talk to people who have had dealings with them. In Chapter 6 we'll look at how you can go about getting to know, and building a good personal relationship with, your opposite number(s).

Concessions

We all make concessions in our everyday lives. For example:

- You agree to give your son some sweets and he agrees to clean his teeth properly

- You agree that your partner's parents can stay over for a few days, and (s)he agrees that you can have a couple of days' fishing or a spa break with your best friend

- A father agrees to take his young daughter to the ice-rink if she agrees to clear up the dishes from dinner

- I agree to do the shopping; my wife agrees that when I get back she'll cook dinner while I watch the football on TV

In all these cases, it's a trade-off: both parties agree to do things they don't really want to do in order to get something they really want. They both make concessions in order to reach agreement.

If you have to negotiate regularly for your organization, you might want to get into the habit, in your daily life, of never giving a concession without getting one in return. If you do that, chances are that it will become second nature for you to act in exactly the same way when you're negotiating.

In any negotiation, both sides are going to have to make some concessions. Neither of you will get everything you want. So part of your preparation should be to plan what concessions you're going to make. Offering concessions does not mean you're weak and ready to keel over and give the other side what they want. Far from it. Concessions are just a signal that you're seriously looking for a compromise – one that will suit both sides. If you stick hard to your key objectives, you can combine firmness with flexibility.

In planning your concessions, cast your net widely. Think broadly about stuff that won't cost you much and that the other side will not expect. If you have been able to identify the other side's key priorities, pick out one area that will help them get closer to achieving their objectives. Within this area, try to come up with one or two concessions that will have minimal impact on your own objectives.

Get into the habit of never giving a concession without getting one in return.

...cont'd

It's a good principle never to give a concession without getting one. In thinking about the concessions you might ask for, think out of the box and consider areas where the other side will not be expecting any demands.

The timing of concessions can be critical. You can – and should – plan in advance what concessions you're prepared to make. But the timing and the presentation – when and how you make the offer – usually has to be decided during the negotiation itself. As with many other aspects of negotiation, a combination of experience and instinct will often give you the answer.

Concessions are best made with reluctance. It can be important to dress them up and to justify them in terms of the other side's interests or problems. If there is one major concession which, having taken everything into account, you are prepared to make in the belief that it will bring the two sides to agreement, hold this in reserve. You can use it as a trump card, presented as a final, closing concession.

In Chapter 10 we'll look at how you can make optimum use of concessions during the actual negotiation.

The timing of concessions can be critical.

Plan your concessions in advance.

Summary

- Have a full understanding of yourself and of the other side

- If you're new to negotiation, take it step-by-step

- Read, talk to colleagues, go along as an observer or assistant before you take the lead

- Rehearse, getting a colleague to play the other side's role

- Learn from previous negotiations with the same party, but remember that some of the key factors may have changed

- If you're part of a team, agree beforehand who will do what

- Make sure you have the key facts and figures at your fingertips

- Prepare your case as a three-tiered pyramid:

    – objective

    – hard information supporting your position

    – underlying interests and concerns

- Try to identify the other side's objective(s), supporting information, and their underlying interests and concerns

- Identify the strengths and weaknesses of your own case

- Plan your concessions in advance

- Never give a concession without getting one

- Give concessions reluctantly and accept them grudgingly

- Hold one major concession in reserve, to be presented as a final, closing concession

6 **Building rapport**

A close personal relationship between the key negotiators can make all the difference in the world. It's worthwhile putting as much (or more) effort into this as you put into preparing your negotiating position. Informal, one-to-one discussions can be more important than the formal negotiating sessions.

A good personal relationship can be the key to success.

Getting to know them

A good personal relationship between the participants is often the key to successful negotiations. It's worthwhile putting as much – or more – effort into building an open, honest relationship with the other side, and strong personal rapport with your opposite number, as you put into preparing your negotiating objectives and position.

The better you know someone, the easier it is to get on with them (OK, there might be the odd exception!). It really is worthwhile making a big effort to get to know the people you'll be negotiating with. If your organization and theirs are already in contact, perhaps working together on some project or other, you may be able to take your time over this, gradually building up the relationship when neither of you is under any pressure. That's the ideal scenario. Personal anecdotes can sometimes be a good way of building a relationship, and you may even be able to use them to make a point. Just make sure they're not too boring!

Getting to know your opposite number(s) means taking a real interest in them as individuals, in their families and in their lives outside the office. Who knows, you might discover a mutual passion for some obscure artist, writer or musician no-one else has ever heard of. If you find that both of you enjoy the same sports or the same kind of movies, you'll have something you can both talk about. It really does not matter what you talk about, but keep it light. A sense of humor can help too.

So take every opportunity to really get to know those you'll be negotiating with. Find out what makes them tick. Then you'll be dealing with them – and they'll be dealing with you – not as anonymous faces across the table, but as real people with individual personalities.

Sometimes you won't have an opportunity to meet your counterparts until you go into the negotiation. If that's the case, make a point of arriving a few minutes early. If you do that, chances are you'll at least be able to exchange a few words with the other side before you get down to the serious business. It might only mean chatting about the weather, or some sensational news you've heard on the radio, or last night's football, or the latest bit of celebrity gossip, but small-talk like this can help to break the ice. Just keep it light, easy and inconsequential. Watch out for body language saying that someone is not the least bit interested, and don't get drawn into expressing personal opinions on sensitive topics like religion or politics.

Use breaks for coffee or lunch to chat to the other side. And don't rush off the moment the meeting's finished. Spend a little time exchanging a few words with your counterpart. It won't cost you anything and it might just help in building that relationship.

Avoid expressing personal opinions on sensitive topics like religion or politics.

One-to-one discussions

Hot tip

Make a point of arriving a few minutes early.

Once trust and mutual respect is established, a quiet chat, one-to-one, with your opposite number can be surprisingly useful. People are often much more relaxed and more prepared to say what they really think if they don't have a large audience. If there's just the two of you – you and your opposite number – you may well find that he or she is prepared to be more open and more honest. And you yourself will probably find it easier to talk about your own concerns and preoccupations if you're talking one-to-one with someone you know and who is on the same wavelength as you.

During the negotiating session itself the other side will almost certainly focus on their organization's objectives and agreed position. If that position has been agreed at a high level they won't have much room for maneuver. They're unlikely to say much, if anything, about what lies behind that position.

In order to have any real chance of persuading them to change that position, you need to probe beneath the surface. You need to understand the pressures they are under and the interests and concerns they are seeking to protect. Almost certainly, you won't be able to do that during the negotiation itself – especially if there are lots of participants. No-one is likely to be too forthcoming in front of an audience.

If you can have a quiet chat, one-to-one, with your counterpart on the other side, you may well find that he or she is prepared to talk far more freely and openly than they would during any formal negotiating session. That might enable you to dig under the surface of what is being said around the conference table – to get at the underlying interests and concerns that explain their position. And that's often the key to progress.

Obviously, if you're going on a fishing expedition of that kind, you'll have to be prepared to say something about the interests and concerns behind your own negotiating position. But that's the name of the game: to negotiate effectively, you have to be prepared give as well as to take.

...cont'd

The more each side knows about the other, the better. The more you understand where the other side are coming from, what concerns they have and what interests they are seeking to protect, the greater your chances of reaching an agreement that satisfies both you and them: a win/win outcome.

Most blockages are freed up and most agreements are made not around the conference table, but in one-to-one meetings.

Informal, one-to-one discussions can help you to dig under the surface of what's being said around the conference table.

Summary

- A good personal relationship between the key negotiators is often the key to success

- Try to get to know the people you'll be dealing with before you sit down to negotiate

- Find out what makes them tick

- Put as much effort into getting to know them as into preparing your case

- Take a real interest in them as individuals: their lives and their families

- Informal one-to-one discussions are often the key to success

- Arrive early and leave late

- Small talk before and after the meeting can help you to get to know the other side

- Getting the other side to change their position means understanding the pressures they are under and the interests they are protecting

7 Presenting your case

In presenting your case it's important to make a strong, positive impact. This chapter describes some of the techniques that can help you to get your message across effectively.

Making an impact

In presenting your case, use the same skills of oral expression you would use if you were delivering a presentation or taking part in a meeting.

It's important to make a personal impact. Speak:

Speak clearly and concisely.

- Clearly

- Concisely

- Confidently

- Fluently

- With energy

- With conviction, and

- Not too fast

Maintain eye contact with your opposite number. If there are several people on the other side, treat them as your audience, making occasional eye contact with each one.

Make eye contact with your opposite number.

Be brisk and businesslike: assertive, but not aggressive. Later we'll look at some of the techniques that can help you to get your points across effectively.

Remember that anything said with great confidence has a good chance of being believed. The other side of the coin is that hesitancy, uncertainty or lack of confidence will reduce the effectiveness of the message, however well-founded it may be, and can destroy belief in what you're saying. Studies have shown that how you speak and the body language you use are at least as important as the content of what you say.

How to begin

Your opening statement needs to be prepared and rehearsed. Use a brief speaking note to remind you of the key points you're going to make. The better prepared you are, the more confident you'll feel; and the more confident you feel, the greater the chance that you will get your message across effectively.

Begin by stressing from the outset the need for agreement, and your determination to achieve a result that's satisfactory to both sides. Demonstrate, in your opening statement, that you're in command of your facts and arguments, and that you know what you're talking about.

When it comes to the substantive subject-matter of the negotiation, it's usually best to begin with stuff that's relatively straightforward and uncontroversial. So focus first on points on which both sides are likely to be able to agree without much difficulty.

Whatever you propose, look at it from the other side's perspective and always concentrate on the benefits to them. For example, if you want to persuade your manager to allow you to go on an expensive training course, you'll probably suggest that it will help you to do your job more effectively. Fair enough, but he or she will probably be more persuadable if you can show that your attendance on the training course will be of real benefit:

1 **To the manager** – because it will enable him or her to delegate more work to you, and will also mean that they will be seen as a manager who cares about developing the skills of their people and is therefore more likely to attract and retain good-quality staff

2 **To the organization** – perhaps by building up its knowledge-base and thereby enabling it to increase productivity or to expand into a new area of activity

If you have done your homework and prepared thoroughly, you should have a sufficient understanding of the other side to be able to phrase your sentences so that they are in tune with their way of thinking. Put yourself in their shoes and ask yourself: what would they like to hear?

Use a brief speaking note to remind yourself of the key points.

Anything said with great confidence has a good chance of being believed.

...cont'd

If your proposals include any complex technical or other details, put them in writing or use a visual aid to explain them.

Explain the thinking behind your proposal. When you have completed your explanation, explain the conditions attached to it. Finish by giving a crisp summary. Then keep quiet. Allow the other side to digest it.

Techniques that can help

- **Repetition:** simply repeating your position or statement again and again can be surprisingly effective

- **Quoting precedents:** the more recent and more relevant, the better

- **Specific examples and anecdotes:** often a good way of illustrating or reinforcing facts and arguments

- **Using "we" rather than "I":** this emphasizes that you are speaking for, and with the authority of, your whole organization

- **Labeling your remarks:** announcing the type of statement you're about to make is a technique often used by experienced negotiators to introduce what follows, using phrases such as:
  "Let me make a suggestion … "
  "I'd like to ask a couple of questions about that …"
  "I'd just like to summarize my understanding of what you're saying …"

- **Expressing feelings:** by commenting from time to time on the thoughts and feelings going through your mind, you will come across as a human being with real emotions. Here are a couple of examples:
  "I'm really concerned that we still seem to be at cross-purposes on this"
  "I'm getting the impression that this concession we've made is seen as a sign of weakness. It's just a real attempt get things moving and to encourage you to offer something in return."

- **Positive body language:** this – and especially eye contact – can be a powerful way of reinforcing your case. We'll look at this in more detail in Chapter 9.

- **The rule of three:** this can be an effective rhetorical device (as shown, for example, by Mrs Thatcher's *"No! No! No!"*), creating a sense of completeness, but don't overdo this

Use specific examples and anecdotes to back up your facts and arguments.

...cont'd

If the other side make an emotional attack, either stay silent or make a calm, factual response.

- **Contrast:** another useful rhetorical device (in presenting your case you might even be able to use an adaptation of George W. Bush's *"You're either with us or you're against us"*)

- **Staying silent:** if the other side make an emotional or unjustified attack, the best thing to do may be to sit there and not say a word. People often feel uncomfortable with silence, especially if they have doubts about what they have said.

If your facts are wrong

We all make mistakes. Occasionally you might find that, despite your best efforts, you have argued a case based on wrong information. If that happens:

1 Don't beat about the bush. Make a straightforward apology

2 Explain that it was a genuine misunderstanding of the facts

3 Revise your proposal, making a new offer based on correct information

4 If you can, find a face-saving formula

Summary

- Use the same skills of oral expression you would use in making a presentation or taking part in a meeting

- Speak clearly, concisely and confidently

- Maintain eye contact with your opposite number

- Make sure your opening statement has been carefully prepared and rehearsed

- Stress your determination to reach agreement

- Show that you are in command of your facts

- Focus first on points on which both sides are likely to agree

- In framing your proposals concentrate on the benefits to the other side

- Put complex technical details in writing or use a visual aid

- Use specific examples and anecdotes to reinforce facts and arguments

- End your presentation with a crisp summary

- Remember the power of silence

8 Scrutinizing their case

The main skills needed when you scrutinize the other side's case are listening and questioning. Neither of these is as easy as it might appear. It's important to listen to every single word and to question everything.

Listen carefully to every single word.

Listening

Listen as if your life depended on it. Listen to every word they say, and take accurate notes. Make sure you have a clear and unambiguous understanding of the other side's position. Without that, you can't negotiate effectively.

If you don't understand anything, speak up. If the other side quote facts or figures that are unclear, it's usually best to jump in immediately with a request for clarification. If the other side's case has a number of discrete elements, it's worthwhile checking your understanding of each element before they move on to the next. You can do this by using your own words to summarize and regurgitate it back to them.

One of the keys to successful negotiations is listening to what is said and seeing behind it – taking in hints or nuances that give you an insight into the thinking or motivation of the other side. That's not always easy, but as with many other aspects of negotiation, the more practice you have, the easier it becomes.

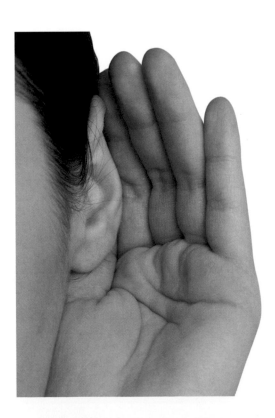

Questioning

Question everything and check every little detail. The more questions you can come up with, the better. The more detail you ask for, the harder it is for the other side to stick to facts, figures or statements that are false or misleading. Challenge and test all their assumptions and conclusions. Are they based on evidence? Ask for proof. If you need time to investigate and check some fact or statement, ask for a break. Consider putting any very detailed or complex questions in writing and inviting the other side to respond in writing at your next meeting.

Focus especially on anything you're unsure or unhappy about, using simple questions to challenge assumptions. Ask open questions – questions that cannot be answered with a "yes" or a "no".

The best words with which to begin a question are usually:

- Why?
- When?
- Who?
- Where
- How?
- What if?

After asking an open question, wait. Sit in silence. Resist the temptation to explain or expand on your question. Just wait for the other side to respond. Silence can be a very powerful tool. Use it. Allow the other side the time to continue giving you the information you need. If you don't wait, you may not get all the facts you need. Make sure you get a complete answer before you move on. Use the power of silence.

If the other side give an incomplete answer or hesitate to finish a sentence, you can say "and?" Don't be in a hurry to move on to your next point until you have got as much mileage as you can out of the question you have already asked. Silence can help you to do that.

Question everything.

Ask open questions.

...cont'd

Take a careful note of any questions being sidestepped. You have probably touched on sensitive areas. You may want to come back to these and perhaps approach them from a different angle.

As the other side speak, try to identify:

● **Areas of overlap** – where their position and yours seems to be identical

● **Areas of proximity** – where the two positions, though not identical, seem to be pretty close

● **Areas of contention** – where there are clearly substantial differences between you

Look really carefully at how the other side make their case. Examine their body language. Look at their gestures and expressions, and the way they sit and move. Does all this reinforce – or contradict – what they are saying?

Eyes are particularly important. If they are not making eye contact, but are looking above you or looking into the distance, that may indicate insincerity, nervousness, uncertainty or lack of conviction.

When the other side have finished presenting their case, don't react immediately – either positively or negatively. Keep your powder dry. Be inscrutable.

Don't get caught out

Untrue facts and statements are the oldest form of trickery. Watch out for them and verify the other side's factual assertions. Watch out for flaws and inconsistencies in the other side's case:

- Errors of fact

- Statistics that are incorrect or misleading

- Errors of logic

- Statements or conclusions that are not supported by evidence

- Inconsistencies or contradictions (for example, between what was said earlier and what is being said now)

If you catch someone out misrepresenting the facts, you have two options:

1 Pull them up straight away. If you're certain of your own facts, you can be strong

2 Let them dig a deeper hole. Save it up for later when you can use it to maximum effect

Using an estimate as if it were an exact figure or dropping crucial words – such as *let's assume*, *for the sake of argument* or *based on* – into the conversation deliberately positioned so that you ignore it, are two ploys to watch out for. You can deal with these tactics by:

- Making it obvious that you give great attention to detail and to every single word

- Making a note and letting the other side know that you are doing this: "Let me just make a note. I'm sure we'll need to refer to that later."

- Checking what you are being told: "Let me be sure I've got this right."

- Querying what's being said: "Are you sure about that? It seems unlikely. In my experience …"

Watch out for untrue facts and statements.

...cont'd

Don't let them blind you with science – incomprehensible statistics or scientific or technical language designed to mystify or mislead. Keep a very close eye on numbers – percentages, discount rates, exchange rates, and so on. These can easily be used to confuse or to gain an advantage. Watch out for graphs, bar-charts or diagrams with scales that emphasize one relatively unimportant factor and skate over a more important one.

If the other side rattles off figures so fast that no-one has a chance to take them in or question them, slow the pace and make sure you fully understand the significance of every single figure. Always check figures and technical details meticulously. If necessary, ask for them to be put in writing and handed over so that you can take them away to study or to refer to a technical expert.

Thorough preparation and having a clear understanding, before you begin the negotiation, of the key statistical and/or technical details is the best safeguard against being bamboozled by ploys of this kind.

If things get difficult

The people on the other side are not always straightforward. They might try to shift the goalposts, perhaps claiming that there is:

- Less money

- Different specifications

- Unexpected competition

- A new company policy with which they must comply

If you're faced with ploys of this kind, be very suspicious. Don't believe in accidents. Be relentless in asking for more and more detail. Ask questions like:

- Why has this problem arisen now – at the last minute, when it's bound to cause problems?

- What's happened to the money allocated to this? When are your budgets set? What financial provisions are there for this kind of operation?

- When was this new policy drawn up? Who was responsible? In what other cases is it being used?

You may not get answers to all these questions, but at least the other side will realize that you have not been taken in.

If they make veiled threats, it's often best to note but ignore them. Only take them seriously if you are in a weak position and you know that they know this. If that's the case, ask yourself:

- Why are they so anxious to get me to agree?

- What have I missed?

...cont'd

If they say something is non-negotiable, there are three possibilities:

1   It really is non-negotiable

2   They think it is non-negotiable, when it is (perhaps someone higher up will give them permission to be more flexible)

3   It's a ploy, intended to close off discussion of that element of the negotiation

If you accept that it really is non-negotiable, you can:

● Test its validity by probing questioning.

● Acknowledge it and move on to other points. If you make real progress on these, the other side may be reluctant to throw away the progress made.

● Open up other avenues that could be explored if this stumbling block was removed.

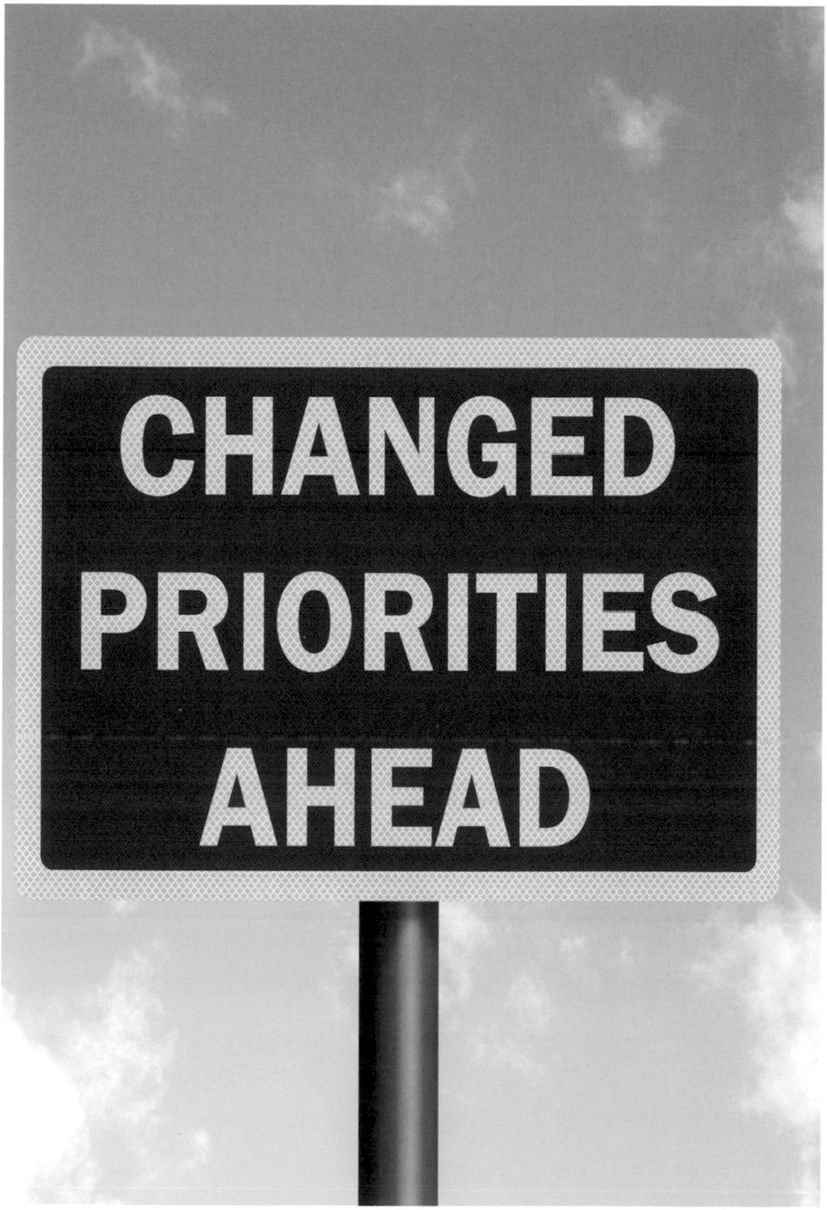
CHANGED
PRIORITIES
AHEAD

Summary

- Listen as if your life depended on it

- If you don't understand anything, speak up

- Question everything and check every little detail

- Ask open questions

- Use the power of silence

- Examine the other side's body language to see whether it reinforces or contradicts what they are saying

- Untrue facts and statements are the oldest form of trickery

- Don't let them blind you with science

- Check figures and technical details meticulously

- Identify areas of overlap and areas of contention

- If they try to shift the goalposts, be very suspicious and ask for more and more detail

9 Body language

Body language – both yours and theirs – is hugely important. If there is conflict between what they see and what they hear, most people will go by what they see. When used effectively, body language can be a powerful additional negotiating tool.

Perception

The way we are perceived owes as much – or more – to our body language as to the words we use. So a good understanding of body language gives you an additional – and often critical - negotiating tool.

For example:

- If you lean or move slightly towards the other person, it may suggest that you are keen to reduce the gap between your negotiating positions. But don't get too close! That could be perceived as a threat.

- If you make someone alter their physical position (for example, by handing them a piece of paper to examine or using a flip-chart to illustrate a point), that may encourage them to think about altering their negotiating position.

- If you're sitting alongside someone, crossing your legs towards them, it may indicate that you're comfortable in their company and want to engage in conversation.

On the other hand, if the other side relax back in the chair, fold their arms and feign interest in other things on the desk, then you have more work to do. If they are alert and upright, then their mind is working and they are thinking it through. If they become relaxed – either it's the green light or a decision has been reached.

We have five senses: sight, sound, touch, taste and smell. Research has shown that we absorb information through these senses in the following very different proportions:

- Sight: 83%

- Sound: 12%

- Touch: 1%

- Taste: 1%

- Smell: 3%

Surprised? Those percentages seem pretty amazing. They show that when it comes to taking in information, seeing is much more powerful than hearing.

Seeing is more powerful than hearing.

If you think about it, perhaps you should not be too surprised. If you listen to a lecture, you'll probably remember one or two bits – especially if the lecturer has had the skill to enliven it with some anecdotes or quotations or a touch of humor. But you'll forget a great deal of it. If you see a visual image – whether it's an object, a drawing, a photograph, a video clip or even a PowerPoint presentation – you're more likely to remember it.

A famous study by Professor Albert Mehrabian came to two main conclusions:

1 Any face-to-face communication consists of three elements: words, tone of voice, and non-verbal behavior (i.e. body language)

2 The non-verbal elements are particularly important for communicating feelings and attitude, and if words disagree with the tone of voice and body language, people are likely to believe the tonality and body language rather than the words

If someone says *"I do not have a problem with you!"* but at the same time avoids eye-contact, looks anxious, and has negative body language, you'll trust the body language rather than the literal meaning of the word.

Watch out for body language that contradicts what is being said.

...cont'd

What this means for a negotiator is that words alone are not enough. If his or her body language conflicts with what is being said, the other side will mistrust the words and go by the body language. So body language is hugely important – both in presenting your own case and in interpreting what the other side say.

In preparing for a negotiation, presenting your case and listening to the other side's case, pay as much attention to body language – and to how both you and they speak – as to the substance of what is said. How you put your points across and the body language you use are as important as the content of what you say. However, don't take all body language at face value. An experienced negotiator might try to fool you. Body language is often a good indicator of mood, but it can sometimes mislead. Over time you'll learn how to interpret it. As you gain in experience you'll learn to trust your instincts.

Eye contact

The single most important element of body language is eye contact. It's an information-conductor, indicating our desire to give and to receive information.

If you're in a negotiation, make eye contact for a few seconds at regular intervals with every person on the other side, but concentrate especially on the team leader and on anyone else whose body language suggests that they are especially sympathetic or interested. If you watch really carefully, you should be able to identify the most receptive listener(s).

The level of your upper eyelid is a good indicator of your level of interest. The higher it is, the greater the interest:

- The level of the upper eyelid is so high that the white of the eye can be seen above the iris and pupil = shock or surprise

- The level of the upper eyelid is between the top of the iris and the top of the pupil = high interest

- The level of the upper eyelid is at the center of the pupil = lowering of interest

- The upper eyelid is below the pupil = boredom or weariness

If you want to show a willingness to change your negotiating position and encourage the other side to change, raise the level of your upper eyelid to the high interest level.

Eye contact and positive body language are really important.

Positive language

Perception is power. High-powered people tend to walk purposefully and to stand and sit upright. As we have already seen, how you're perceived – the impact you make on the other side – owes as much to your body language as to what you have to say. You can do a lot to heighten the impact you make by making sure that your body language is positive and supports, rather than contradicts, the words coming out of your mouth. Here are some examples of positive body language:

- Standing or sitting with body facing the other person

- Head lifted in interest

- An open, friendly expression

- Direct eye contact

- A relaxed but alert posture

- Legs and arms uncrossed

- Hands palm up and on show

- A smile may soften the ambience and change the tone of the meeting. Sometimes it can be used to stimulate comments or questions or to encourage the giving of more information

An open posture and positive body language suggests:

- Willingness to listen

- Interest

- Openness of mind

- A feeling of confidence and strength

Negative language

Conversely, if your body language contradicts what you're saying, it can seriously damage your credibility and undermine your arguments. Examples of negative body language include:

- An indirect or evasive gaze, perhaps looking at the ceiling or out the window = shifty and/or lacking confidence

- Fidgeting, pulling their ear = uncomfortable

- Smiling unnecessarily or inappropriately (especially when combined with speaking very quickly) = nervous and lacking confidence

- Arms crossed = defensive

- Standing or sitting with the body facing away from the other person = rigid

- Hands hidden or palms down = defensive

- Yawning, doodling, leaning back in chair = bored

- Head down, eyes partly closed or constantly looking away = distracted

Mirroring

A technique used by some negotiators is that of mirroring – reflecting the way the other side behave. This is based on the premise that we are subconsciously more at ease with people who are similar to ourselves. Mirroring the other side's body language can create an impression of empathy. Usually, the more empathetic you are and the better you get on with the other side, the greater your chances of achieving a successful, win/win result.

You can mirror:

- **Dress:** aim to dress as formally or informally as they do

- **Posture:** if they sit upright, so do you

- **Voice:** listen carefully to how they speak – the speed and tone of their voice – and respond in a similar way. For example, do they speak concisely or at great length? In responding, you can take your cue from them

- **Use of eyes, hand gestures and other body language:** you can mirror their actions

- **Mood:** you can pick up on their attitude and react in a similar vein. For example, are they deadly serious or are their comments accompanied by a little humor?

Summary

- The way we are perceived depends mainly on body language

- In taking in information, seeing is much more powerful than hearing

- Body language is especially important for communicating feelings and attitudes

- If there is conflict between the body language and the words, most people will trust the body language

- Eye contact is the most important element of body language

- Make eye contact for a few seconds at regular intervals with every person on the other side

- Use positive body language to heighten the impact of your words

- Consider whether the other side's body language supports or contradicts what they are saying

- Mirroring the other side's behavior can help to create an impression of empathy

10 Tactics

This chapter looks at some of the tactical issues that can arise during a negotiation. Every negotiation is different and experience is often the best guide. Learning by doing is the best way to develop tactical awareness.

Kicking off

Aim high to begin with.

How do you want to begin the negotiation? Speak first? Or let the other side begin, so that you can listen to their proposals and then respond?

Sometimes it may be out of your hands. But sometimes you'll have a choice. If that's the case, consider the pros and cons carefully.

If you speak first, you'll be able to:

- Set the tenor

- Control the initial exchanges

- Focus on those elements that are of greatest importance to you

If the other side speak first:

- You'll be in a better position to counter their arguments

- You'll be able to adjust your position in the light of what you've heard. For example, if it becomes clear that the gap between the two sides is smaller than you expected, you can make a response which is closer to them than your own opening proposal would have been

If you make the opening proposal, aim high to begin with. Research has shown that it pays to open with a high initial proposal. Always ask for much more than you expect to get, and offer much less than you expect to have to give. If you open with what you consider a fair offer, there is a danger that the other side

will regard it as an opening gambit, and assume that you would be prepared to settle for a good deal less. If you begin high, you have a better chance of ending up with something you can accept.

But flexibility is essential. You'll have to think on your feet. And you'll almost certainly need to adjust what you're offering and what you're demanding as the negotiations proceed and reality kicks in.

In the early stages don't suggest that your position is inviolate, or try to pin down the other side to a fixed position. Both sides need room for maneuver. So don't force them into a corner or into making promises that could reduce their options later.

Get the other side to table all their demands at the same time, so that you can link them together and consider each element in the context of the overall agreement. Then:

1 First, look for areas of commonality: areas where the two sides agree or are very close

2 Next, identify minor points where you can concede something

3 Finally, identify areas where there are major differences

Then you can revisit your proposal (or your response) and consider whether you need to make some minor adjustments or to have a major rethink.

Precedent

The power of precedent often wins. You may hear phrases like:

- *"We've always done it like this. No way can we change."*

- *"If you're going to move the goal-posts by tearing up the precedent, we'll have to renegotiate or look elsewhere."*

- *"There was a good reason for the precedent. Our whole operation relies on that way of operating."*

If you want to use precedent to support your case, you may be able to rely on:

- A previous written agreement or contract

- Previous papers: root out, as part of your preparation, any relevant letters, emails, memos, faxes, etc. that you might want to quote

- De facto precedent: "It has been done this way in the past" (perhaps only once!)

- Implicit or intended precedent: in the spirit of the agreement

- The industry standard

If you want to resist the use of precedent, you may be able to argue that:

- This is a unique situation, negotiation or circumstance

- Times change: the precedent has been overtaken by events and is out-of-date

- That case was a special one-off agreement and never constituted a precedent: it was for a fixed term; or the circumstances were unique

Concessions

Trading concessions is a key part of negotiation. Give them reluctantly and accept them grudgingly. Never make a concession easily or quickly, and always attach your own conditions. Indicate that every concession you make is a substantial loss. Spell out the detailed implications for you – and make sure the other side understand them.

It's often best to hold back concessions and link them to something you want. If negotiating on a number of related items, link them together so that you can make concessions on those of least importance in order to gain extra leverage for your main objective. Negotiating a package also makes it easier to find out the other side's real priorities.

Accept concessions grudgingly and make them look insubstantial to you. If you can gain a concession you don't really want, it can often be traded back later for something you do want. Look for opportunities for horse-and-cart linkages of concessions, using one to prompt a further concession with a logical link to the first: "If you are going to do that, then surely it makes sense to …"

You can make conditional proposals, along the lines of: "If you are prepared to do X, we will consider doing Y" or "If you pay transportation costs, we'll see if we can manage earlier delivery." In doing this:

- Present the condition first

- Make it firm and strong, using a word like "do"

- Make your part of the bargain more tentative, using a word like "consider"

Don't be fooled by "extra" concessions that the other side may offer. If you're booking a hotel room you might be quoted a top rate for a luxury room with a suite and extras such as fruit and flowers in the room, free mineral water, newspapers, breakfast, complimentary welcome drinks, and so on. If you don't attach much value to those extras, you'll get better value for money by booking a standard room at the best rate you can get.

...cont'd

Make conditional proposals: "if you ... I'll consider ...".

Remember that the other side's values are not your values. So minimize the value of any extra concession you're offered. You can often remove or greatly reduce its value by saying things like:

- "I don't need it"

- "I would expect that to be included anyway"

- "It's not worth much to me"

Use of the conditional "yes" has been described as the cornerstone of effective negotiation. If you're going to say yes to something, think about what else you can ask for at the same time. You can use phrases such as "Yes, provided that includes…" or "Yes, and I assume that…" If, for example, you are buying a basic item or service, think about what additional stuff you can ask the supplier to include. They'll cost him much less than they would cost you.

Visualize a set of scales and put a weight on every concession you get and every one you give. List the two sides on a sheet of paper. Make sure it either balances or tips in your favor!

When you've reached the point where any further concessions would drive you down below your bottom line, revisit the whole agreement and draw attention to the concessions you have already made. Make the other side see the difference between your original position and where you are now.

Have a trump card up your sleeve – something that is valuable to the other side, not necessarily to you – and hold it in reserve until you can use it to conclude the agreement. This is how it works:

1   Identify a key objective of the other side which you know you can satisfy

2   Say early on in the negotiation that you can't possibly satisfy it

3   Be reluctant even to discuss it

4   Make your other concessions on a decreasingly small scale, giving the other side less and less room for maneuver

5   Hint at, but withhold, your trump card: "I would really like to .... but I can't see how we could possibly ..."

6   Then play what if: "But in the unlikely event that .... What would you offer in return?"

7   Make sure that all other elements of your stance are in place to satisfy your key objectives

8   Play your trump card – the thing you identified that you know will help the other side achieve a key objective – making it clear that this is a final "now or never" offer

9   Finalize the negotiation as soon as you can

Timing – knowing when to play your trump card – is critical. Play it too soon and you will lose the initiative over subsequent elements of the negotiation. If you leave it until it's too late, the other side may have lost interest in reaching agreement with you, and perhaps started to look elsewhere.

Keep one trump card up your sleeve.

Beware

Don't assume their understanding is the same as yours.

Check as you go along

Witnesses to an accident or a crime often give conflicting accounts. Everyone interprets what they see slightly differently. It's just the same in a negotiation. Don't assume that their interpretation of what has been agreed is the same as yours. Negotiations at the very highest levels sometimes break up with different participants having a rather different understanding of what has been agreed. You can avoid this by checking details regularly as you go along to ensure that your understanding is the same as theirs. Regular summarizing of your assessment of positions is a good way to do this.

Put yourself in their shoes

Putting yourself in the other side's shoes – not just now and again, but regularly and frequently throughout the negotiation – will help you to judge how to frame your proposal and responses. If there are several people in the other side's team it's often best to focus on one individual. Change viewpoint and look at things not from your own perspective, but from that of:

● The other side

● An objective external observer

Can you imagine what would be going through their minds? What would they think about your proposals and reactions? What would they think about your feelings?

By examining the facts and arguments from the other side's point of view, and from that of an impartial observer, you may be able to obtain additional information and insights and to build rapport.

Stepping back from the detail – like a painter who steps back to look at his picture from a different angle or a greater distance – can help you to get an overall impression of how the negotiation is going and to identify the strengths and weaknesses of your case.

Dealing with difficult people

Not everyone you negotiate with will want a win/win result. Sometimes – especially if it's a one-off negotiation and the two parties are unlikely to have to deal with one another again – the other side will want to get the better of you.

If the other side play hardball, don't roll over and let them walk all over you. Don't pretend that the gap between you is smaller than it really is. You can't buy a good relationship by ignoring substantive differences or by making unjustified concessions. Appeasement does not work.

The lack of any military response to German occupation of Czechoslovakia in 1939 probably encouraged Hitler to believe that his invasion of Poland would not lead to war. Similarly, any attempt to appease or buy off the other side by giving in to some of their demands, in the hope that this will enable you to avoid major concessions, is almost certainly misguided.

A negotiator who tries to bully you into accepting something that's clearly unacceptable is likely to regard any concession as a sign of weakness. You may think that if you make an unjustified concession now, it will encourage the other side to make a concession next time; they are more likely to believe that if they are stubborn enough, you will give in again. The best way to deal with a bully – someone who is hell-bent on getting everything and leaving you with nothing – is to stand up to him (or her).

Don't give in to the other side if they suggest that failure to go along with their unreasonable demands will threaten your future relationship with them. Good relationships depend upon mutual trust and respect. Try to separate the people from the problem and to deal with the substantive issues on their merits. Don't give in for the purpose of seeking to improve the relationship. If, at the end of the day, you're able to achieve an outcome that is recognized as good by both parties, this will strengthen, rather than weaken, the relationship.

If the other side adopt a hostile, confrontational approach, resist the temptation to respond in kind. If you do act in that way it may, if anything, encourage them to believe that this is the only way to behave. It's much better if you can model the kind of friendly, rational behavior you want the other side to show.

Summary

- Consider the pros and cons of making, or letting the other side make, the opening proposal

- Ask for more than you expect to get, and offer less than you expect to have to give

- Get the other side to table all their demands at the same time

- Identify areas of commonality, areas where there are minor differences and areas where there are major differences

- Remember the power of precedent

- Trading concessions is a key part of negotiation

- Give concessions reluctantly and accept them grudgingly

- Make conditional proposals

- Make sure the concessions you get are worth at least as much as those you give

- Identify one key concession and hold it in reserve as a trump card you can use to conclude the agreement

- During the negotiation regularly put yourself in the shoes of the other side

11 Practicalities

Practical arrangements can sometimes have a disproportionate effect on the outcome of a negotiation. So it's important to pay careful attention to the physical arrangements and other practicalities.

First impressions are important.

Introduction

Physical arrangements and other practicalities can have an important effect on the outcome of any negotiation. Sometimes you'll be able to control these and sometimes you won't. But it's always worthwhile giving them some thought and attention in advance.

First impressions are important. So think about how you wish to be perceived. Dress carefully: you need to feel comfortable and to be smart. Power dressing can denote confidence and authority and may earn respect, but can carry negative connotations of aggression. If in doubt, dress conservatively. You might want to think about your accessories, such as briefcase, laptop or other gadgetry, watch, shoes, ties, jewelry, socks, handbag, etc. They all contribute to the way you and your organization are seen. Perception can be as important as reality.

Venue

Holding the negotiation on your own premises has a number of advantages:

- You can draw up the agenda and arrange the seating

- You will have easy access to any back-up you may need (colleagues or papers you might want to consult)

- You can control the environment to suit you (temperature of the room, timing of breaks, etc.)

- You may have fewer problems if you need to prolong the meeting (the other side will have the inconvenience of a delayed journey home)

However, an offer to meet on the premises of the other party can sometimes pay dividends. It suggests that you are flexible, you want to make an effort to help the other side, and you're keen to reach an agreement. If your counterpart is new to negotiation or feels insecure for some other reason, you might want to give him or her the security of proximity to staff or colleagues. If you want to feel free to end the meeting by walking away, this will probably be easier in the other party's office.

If both parties to the negotiation are extremely busy and likely to be subjected to frequent interruptions, it may make sense to meet on neutral ground where seclusion can be guaranteed. Neither party will have the advantage of familiarity with their surroundings; and both will need to ship in any experts or material they need.

Wherever you meet, make sure the room has all the facilities you'll need. It's often better to avoid using visual aids in a negotiation: they can interrupt the flow of discussion and act as a barrier between the participants. But if used sparingly, a flip chart, whiteboard or laptop/tablet computer can sometimes be useful to convey complex information or to illustrate a technical point. If you do want to use some kind of visual aid, check that the room has these facilities.

...cont'd

A change of venue can sometimes help to produce a change in attitudes.

The side hosting the meeting may sometimes seek to use subtle or not-so-subtle props to impress, intimidate or put pressure on the other side. Examples of this are lavish reception areas, meeting rooms or offices; framed photographs of the organization's senior people with statesmen or other VIPs; prominently displayed lists of big-name clients; photographs of major projects they've been involved in; details of international offices and affiliates; competitors' literature deliberately left where it can be seen; and other such ploys. If you come up against tricks of this kind, don't be over-impressed or intimidated.

Seating

Always find out in advance exactly who will be attending. You'll be at a disadvantage if you're outnumbered. Try to make sure that the size of your team matches the other side's.

Each party sitting on opposite sides of an oblong table is the traditional seating plan for a negotiation, and this is often the best option. It emphasizes the separate identities of the two parties.

A team leader who sits at the head of the table may wish to create the impression that they control the proceedings; while informal seating using a round table may help to soften hardline attitudes that are proving a hindrance.

If you are negotiating as a member of a team, it's important that the seating arrangements allow you to make eye contact with other members of your team as well as with the other side.

Occasionally negotiators may seek to gain an advantage by the way seating is arranged. One ploy is to place the opposition in direct sunlight. One Minister I used to work for always used to seat himself in a throne-like chair that was higher than the other chairs in his room. Presumably he felt that by towering above everyone else physically he was reinforcing his position and putting himself in a better position to dominate the discussion. Another Minister used to place his interlocutor at the far end of an oblong table placed in the middle of, and at right angles to, his desk.

So the seating arrangements may suggest that the negotiations are expected to be confrontational, informal, or dominated by your hosts. Once you gauge the tone, you can adapt your approach accordingly. If you're unhappy with the seating arrangements, get them changed!

It's almost always counter-productive to seek to gain a negotiating advantage by giving the other side a difficult physical environment. If they think you're giving them a tough time over the seating, they might feel like giving you a tough time over the substance of the negotiation. It's much better if both sides treat each other with respect. If you're both comfortably seated, you'll both feel at ease. And that kind of relaxed atmosphere is more conducive to a constructive discussion.

You'll be at a disadvantage if you're outnumbered.

Ensure you can make easy eye contact with other members of your team.

Agenda and time-frame

It's important to agree beforehand exactly how the negotiation will be conducted. It's always best to agree a definite time-frame. A deadline helps to concentrate the discussion and to minimize irrelevant or long-winded contributions. If you have agreed to meet on the premises of the other party, you might be able to use this concession to your advantage by holding out for a start and finish time that suits you.

If the negotiation will cover several elements it's always best to have an agenda. This will help to define the purpose of the discussion and to focus on the key aspects. Agree beforehand what will be discussed and what will be left out, and use headings that are clear, specific, unchallenging and non-confrontational. Bear in mind that the purpose of the meeting is not to air grievances, but to achieve solutions. It's best to allocate a time period for each item; the order of the agenda and the amount of time allocated should reflect the priority of each item. Specify a time for the meeting to end. Send the agenda out in advance.

Provide water, paper and pencils; have tea and coffee available during breaks; and if it's an all-day meeting lay on sandwiches and soft drinks for the lunch break.

About 90 minutes is the optimum length of time for any negotiating session without a break. If it's allowed to run on beyond that, tiredness and tetchiness may begin to take their toll. A ten- or fifteen-minute break allows participants to use the bathroom, attend to any urgent phone messages, have a coffee and recharge their batteries.

Note-taking

Experienced negotiators ensure that detailed written minutes of the proceedings are taken. It's important to take accurate notes. How this is done will depend upon the size of the negotiating team. With three or more people it's often best to allocate responsibility for note-taking to one individual. In a two-person team it's usually best to share the job: one person speaks while the other takes notes. If you are on your own, you'll have to do the best you can to combine several roles:

- Speaking

- Listening to, and watching, the other side

- Thinking

- Taking notes

It's not easy, but with experience you will learn to identify the key points that need to be recorded. The closer to verbatim your notes are, the better. You'll need to record especially:

- Key elements of the other side's proposals

- Facts or figures quoted by the other side which you may want to challenge or question

- Any flaws in the other side's argumentation

- Points agreed

- Action points (exactly what action is to be taken, by whom and by when)

Negotiating at a distance

Face-to-face negotiation is best. If you're sitting around the same table as your counterpart, there's a much better chance that you'll be able to establish some kind of personal rapport. Body language – both yours and the other side's – will come into play. It will be easier to judge the effect your proposals have on the other side – and vice versa. Seeing, as well as hearing, one another's reactions will give both of you more information and help to inform your judgment.

Sometimes, however, geographical constraints or tight schedules mean that you have to negotiate at a distance. If that's the case, it's important to prepare at least as thoroughly as you would for a face-to-face negotiation.

If you're signing a straightforward contract, you might simply be able to look it over – or get your legal adviser to look it over – sign it, and send it back in the post. If you want to suggest some changes, you can probably do that by email. That's how I handled the contract for writing this book.

Sometimes, because of the urgency or the limited availability of the key people, you may have to negotiate by telephone. That's not the best negotiating scenario, but sometimes it's unavoidable. It may be, for example, that most elements of a negotiation have been agreed at a face-to-face meeting, but that it did not prove possible to finalize all the details in the time available. In those circumstances it may suit both sides to resolve the outstanding points by telephone.

The fact that you cannot see the person at the other end of the line has many disadvantages. But it also has some advantages. You can refer easily to your notes: so keep them close at hand, and set out in a form that makes it easy for you to find the information, the arguments and the questions you'll want to use during your conversation.

Lack of visual contact with your opposite number can help you to concentrate fully on what is being said and how it's being said. Pauses and the intonation and quality of the voice can tell us something about the other party. Watch out for words and phrases such as "incidentally" and "by the way" which are sometimes used to camouflage important information.

Dewsbury Library

Tel: (01484) 414 868
Email: Dewsbury.lic@kirklees.gov.uk

Customer ID: *****9686

Items that you have borrowed

Title: Effective negotiations in easy steps
ID: 800420869
Due: 14 June 2022

Total items: 1
Checked out: 1
Overdue: 0
Hold requests: 0
Ready for collection: 0
24/05/2022 10:42

Thank you for using the bibliotheca SelfCheck System.
We hope to see you soon.

www.kirklees.gov.uk/community/libraries

...cont'd

If you do find yourself having to negotiate over the phone, it's imperative to confirm immediately in writing exactly what has been agreed, and to get the other side's written confirmation and acceptance of this. With most organizations now using email as a standard means of communication, this can be done much more easily and quickly than was once the case.

Summary

- Practicalities and physical arrangements can affect the outcome of a negotiation

- Consider the pros and cons of holding the negotiation on your premises, on the premises of the other side, or on neutral ground

- Make sure the room you're going to use has all the facilities you need

- Give careful attention to seating arrangements

- Agree a definite time frame

- If the negotiation will cover several elements, agree an agenda

- Make sure there are breaks every 90 minutes or so

- Ensure detailed and accurate notes are taken

- Record key points in notes that are as close as possible to verbatim

12 Multi-party negotiations

Most of the advice in this book applies as much to multi-party as to bilateral negotiations. But there are some additional things you'll need to bear in mind. You'll have to give even more time and attention to developing good personal relationships with the other participants. If it's an international negotiation, you'll need to be aware of, and to respect, cultural differences.

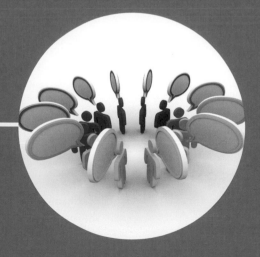

Preparation and tactics

For any multi-party negotiation it's important to be clear about the negotiating process: to understand exactly what the time-frame is, how the discussions will be conducted and how decisions will be taken. There is likely to be a pre-arranged agenda, but working procedures can vary a good deal depending on the type of negotiations.

Negotiating with more than one party presents both problems and opportunities. Getting a good understanding of the negotiating objectives and the underlying interests and concerns of just one party on the other side of the table can be difficult enough. When you are dealing with several parties, it's a pretty daunting task. But the key principles of effective negotiating are exactly the same:

- Clear objectives

- Thorough preparation

- Good personal relationships

Preparation for a negotiation in which several parties will participate, each of them fighting their own corner, striving to protect their own interests and achieving their own specific, and often rather different, objectives, involves the same kind of research and investigation as a simple bilateral negotiation. It just means that you need to replicate the process for each of the participating parties. Not easy, but not impossible. In doing this research, try to identify those parties whose objectives and interests:

- Seem fairly close to your own: these are potential allies with whom you may be able to work in seeking an outcome which is satisfactory both to you and to them;

- Are difficult or impossible to reconcile with your own: these parties will be hostile to your objectives and you may need to handle them carefully.

At the outset there will probably be an opportunity for all the participants to outline their overall approach. The meeting will then move on to detailed discussion of the proposed agreement, section by section. This discussion may take the form of a tour de

Don't forget

Good personal relationships are even more important than in a bilateral negotiation.

table, with each participant speaking in turn. Or it may be a free-for-all, with the floor being given to any participant who expresses a wish to speak. In this case, there are two options to consider:

- Get in early to:

    - Set the agenda

    - Steer the discussion in the direction you want it to go

    - Focus on those aspects that are of particular importance to you

    - Get across some key facts or arguments which could affect others' interventions

    - Convince waverers

- Come in late if you:

    - Think others will make some of your points (so that you can concentrate on others)

        Want to hear others' arguments first, so you can counter them

    - Believe you may pick up important information from another intervention

    - Want to appear statesmanlike by summarizing what others have said and drawing conclusions

Based on what you know about the issues, about how the negotiation is going to be handled, and – not least – about the other people around the table, you have to decide which tactics will enable you to make your case most effectively. Experience and instinct are your best guides.

In a multi-party negotiation it's usually best if all the parties are open from the outset about their bottom lines.

Friends and allies

If you are the only one at the table who is arguing your case and seeking the specific outcome that will meet your objectives, it's likely to be pretty difficult. Unless there are special factors which persuade the others to go along with you, your chances of getting what you want are slim, to say the least. I've been in that position myself, when I represented the UK at one of the European Union Council Working Groups in Brussels. At that time there were just 15 EU Member States. Heaven knows what it must be like now, when there are 28 Member States, each with their own agendas, interests and concerns.

In order to stand any chance of achieving a satisfactory result from a multi-party negotiation, you're likely to need some allies; the more allies you have, the greater your chances of success. Alliances are never set in stone. Lord Palmerston (Britain's Prime Minister in the 1850s and 1860s) put his finger on this when he said: "We have no eternal allies and we have no perpetual enemies. Our interests are eternal." In a complex international negotiation alliances may vary from one element of the negotiation to another and they may well change over time, perhaps in response to political changes or economic developments.

Any multi-party negotiation – whether it's an international government-to-government treaty, some other kind of international agreement (e.g. between scientific or academic institutions) or a commercial agreement between companies who want to work together (either on one specific project or more permanently) – is likely to have a number of distinct elements. The approach of each participant to each element may well be different, and it may be that no-one else shares your own approach to every single element. You might therefore need to form different alliances for different aspects of the negotiation.

The importance of alliances in multi-party negotiations means that good personal relationships are, if anything, even more important than in conventional, two-party negotiations. In order to have a good chance of getting your points accepted during the formal negotiating sessions, you'll almost certainly have to pave the way in informal, often bilateral, chats with your opposite numbers. In a multilateral negotiation most participants will be reluctant to reveal more than their basic positions when speaking in front of the whole group. A quiet one-to-one chat is often the way to find out what lies behind their formal positions; to find out what their underlying interests and concerns are.

Networking and doing all you can to get to know your opposite numbers is vitally important. Establishing close personal contacts with your counterparts is not an optional extra; it's an essential pre-requisite for success.

Make sure you have some friends and allies.

Making an impact

In a multi-party negotiation it can be particularly important to make a personal impact when you speak. Here are some key tips:

● Secure a good seating position – so that you can see all the other participants and they can see you

● Look alert and ready to contribute

● Speak clearly and succinctly

● Focus on a small number of key points that are of real importance to you

● Maintain eye contact

● Speak with energy and conviction – and not too fast

● Build on others' contributions (if you can link what you say to what someone else has said, even if you agree with only one small element of their position, this suggests a consensual approach)

● Be positive and constructive (if you have to say "no" to something, try to suggest circumstances or conditions which might enable you to consider saying "yes")

As in any other type of negotiation, you need to listen very carefully to what others say, and take notes of key points or comments. If you don't understand something, ask questions and seek clarification. When you speak yourself, try to use specific examples to back up your arguments.

Cultural differences

If you are taking part in an international negotiation you'll need to take account of cultural differences. These can be quite tricky. There can be significant differences between the beliefs, customs, attitudes and habits of people of different nationality in a whole range of areas. Here are some examples of things which can vary significantly from one country to another:

Tread carefully if you're unsure about the conventions of the people you're negotiating with.

- Language

- Greeting conventions

- Use of first names

- Body language

- Attitudes to personal space

- Religious attitudes

- Attitudes to alcohol and smoking

- Sense of humor

- Eating conventions

- Attitudes to time

- Giving and receiving presents

- How women are regarded and treated

- Attitudes to health and safety issues

It's important to recognize and respect these differences. If you're not familiar with the habits, attitudes, and conventions of the people you're negotiating with, tread very carefully. Remember, too, that we are all individuals and that national stereotypes can sometimes be misleading.

If you're negotiating with people from other countries, don't assume that the negotiation will be in English. If it's a formal international negotiation, you'll probably have professional interpretation, either simultaneous or consecutive. If that's not the case, find out in advance whether it will be acceptable to use English. It can be important to make it clear that you are not assuming that the negotiation will be in English.

...cont'd

If it is agreed that English will be used, try to find out how fluently it is spoken. You'll need to speak more slowly and more clearly than usual; to avoid colloquialisms; and to steer clear of humor, which often does not work across national boundaries and may be misunderstood or misinterpreted. Ideally (even if English is to be used) include in your team someone who speaks the language(s) of the other participants.

There can be many cultural differences apart from language. Let's look at a few examples. In India talking about friends and family is regarded as an important part of establishing a business relationship. In some parts of the world (for example, Saudi Arabia, China, Japan, parts of South-East Asia) saving face can be extremely important. So you may need to concede a point rather than risk humiliating your counterpart.

When working recently in West Africa (Nigeria and Cameroon) I soon discovered that the local approach to time-keeping and punctuality was, to say the least, relaxed. It would have been counter-productive for me to insist on the same standards I would have expected in London or New York. The events in which I was participating were also conducted with much greater formality and respect for hierarchy than would have been the case in London. I had to adapt to the local culture.

An invitation to dinner in Madrid or in Buenos Aires is unlikely to see you sitting down to eat before ten o'clock at the very earliest. When I worked in Moscow I soon discovered that no official luncheon, reception or dinner was complete without multiple toasts and, invariably, lots of vodka (When in Rome ...).

At the EU meetings I attended in Brussels there were often differences of approach between those from northern Europe and those from the south. Those of us from the north would typically plan our interventions in advance, often using a brief speaking note to keep us on track. In contrast, my colleagues from southern Europe would sometimes do it the other way round, using the spoken word as a means of thinking through the issue and formulating their thoughts.

You can compare and contrast the brash negotiating style favored by some Americans with the more indirect style of communication and negotiation favored by some Japanese. But in both cases it's not difficult to find individual examples that contradict these stereotypes.

Thorough preparation can help you to find out about cultural differences before a negotiation. You can read newspapers and magazines and use libraries. You can go on the internet. Perhaps best of all, you can talk to friends or colleagues who have experience of the culture(s) concerned.

It's always worthwhile questioning your assumptions about cultural differences. Don't assume that the people you are negotiating with are either just like you or are totally different. We are all affected by a hundred and one different factors of our upbringing, environment and culture. Nationality can provide important clues about cultural differences, but remember that we are all individuals.

Summary

- Make sure you understand how the negotiation will be conducted and how decisions will be taken

- The same principles apply as in bilateral negotiations:
  - clear objectives
  - thorough preparation
  - good personal relationships

- Networking and good personal relationships are especially important

- Try to identify those parties whose positions are:
  (a) close to your own and
  (b) hostile to your own

- Weigh up the pros and cons of getting in early or coming in late

- Form alliances with those whose aims and objectives are closest to your own

- Keep a careful eye on those whose aims and objectives are likely to be incompatible with yours

- Speak clearly and succinctly to make a strong personal impact

- Don't assume that your own customs and attitudes are shared by others

- Respect cultural differences

13 Closure

The final stages of a negotiation are often the most critical. It's important to make sure that every little element is correct and in place. Make quite sure that you're happy with what has been agreed, and that your organization will be able to implement the agreement.

Take a great deal of care over the final stages.

Final steps

Don't rush the final stages of the negotiation. If one side or the other are under time pressure (for example, because they have a plane to catch) it can be tempting to skate over details that might seem unimportant but could turn out to be really troublesome. So take as much care over the final little elements of your agreement as you've taken over the major issues.

You need to be sure that both sides have full authority to sign up to the agreement. If there's a need for final clearance with a third party, such as the company chairman or Board, partners or lawyers, this needs to made clear.

If you're making a final offer with the intention of closing the negotiation:

● Make sure the atmosphere and the mood of the other side is conducive to agreement – timing can be critical

● Praise – but don't patronize – the other side

● Be self-deprecating: "I haven't had any brilliant new ideas, but ..."

● Emphasize areas of agreement and progress made

● Emphasize the benefits to the other side

● Increase the urgency and firmness of your voice

● Create the impression of decisiveness by gathering up your papers (and perhaps even standing up)

If they resist closure:

● Put yourself in their shoes and try to understand their reluctance

● Say that you will welcome any constructive suggestion or proposal

● Emphasize that you want an agreement acceptable to both sides: win/win

● Give them an escape route. Ask "What if ..." questions

Never say your proposal is final when it is not. Beware of crying wolf.

Once agreement has been reached:

1 Check that everyone has the same understanding of exactly what has been agreed

2 Read over your notes and summarize what's been agreed, item by item

3 Get the other side to agree the precise wording of your summary

4 Define any ambiguous terminology

5 Spell out the terms and conditions so that they are clearly understood by both sides

6 Include action points – spell out exactly what action is to be taken, by whom and by when

7 Have detailed minutes drawn up immediately after the meeting

8 Send the minutes to the other side and ask for written confirmation that's it's an accurate record of the result of the negotiation

9 Circulate this record as quickly as you can: if there is any confusion, misunderstanding or disagreement about what's been agreed, it can be resolved immediately

Check that everyone's understanding of what's been agreed is the same.

Get the other side's written confirmation of the outcome.

Implementation

Implement what's been agreed. If you don't, you can be sure that it will be remembered next time you negotiate with the same people! Brief the people who will be responsible for putting what has been agreed into effect. Ensure that your organization has the necessary skills and resources. Make sure that tasks, responsibilities and deadlines are crystal clear. Agree the order in which action will be taken, and use a Gannt chart to plan the time schedule for each activity. Ensure rigorous monitoring and regular progress reports.

Don't forget

Make sure your organization implements what's been agreed.

Gantt Chart

	January	February	March	April	May
Activity A					
Activity B					
Activity C					
Activity D					
Activity E					

Negotiation check list

Purpose of negotiation

Ideal outcome

Fall-back position

Bottom line

BATNA

Key facts and figures

Killer arguments

Key individuals

Supportive:

Hostile:

Uncertain:

Summary

- Don't rush the final stages of the negotiation

- Make sure both sides have full authority to sign up to the agreement

- Take care over the timing of your final offer

- Check that everyone's understanding of what has been agreed is the same

- Have detailed minutes drawn up immediately after the meeting and get the other side's written confirmation that it is an accurate record

- Make sure your organization has the skills and the resources to implement what has been agreed

- Make sure that tasks and deadlines are clearly defined

- Ensure rigorous monitoring

14 Tricks of the trade

Every trade under the sun has its own little secrets – things an experienced practitioner may do or say to help get the desired result. This chapter covers some of the techniques that a negotiator can use to gain an advantage over, or to avoid being taken in by, the other side.

Tricks of the trade

Some of the stuff that follows has been touched on in other chapters, but it's worthwhile collating and reiterating some of the key stratagems, techniques and ploys that can be used to gain an advantage. They are not always appropriate or feasible, but most of these have been tried and tested and found to work where it counts – in a real negotiation.

Silence
Use the power of silence after a closing question. Look the person in the eye and wait. Don't break the silence. If they don't know the answer, or if they do but don't want to tell you, let them sweat!

Using feelings and emotions
Sometimes it's useful to tell the other side what you are feeling. For example: "I'm beginning to feel that we're not really talking about the same thing" or "I'm getting the impression that we're not going to make any progress on this until we can firm up those figures." Expressing feelings in this way helps you to be seen as an individual with normal human emotions.

Although emotional outbursts should be avoided, a very occasional flash of emotion can help to convince the other side of your honesty and strength of feeling. But use this tactic sparingly.

Getting in quickly
Pitching in quickly and seizing the initiative by being the first to summarize can give you an intangible edge. You are in the driving seat: you're in control; you're setting the pace; and you're establishing the agenda for the ensuing discussion.

Playing the other side's words back to them
Occasionally you may be able to play the other side's words back to them – but subtly rewording what they have said in order, without altering the facts, to weaken their position or strengthen your own. For example, if they say "So you will arrange transport" you might respond: "So you can't take on responsibility for arranging transport." This leaves the door open for you to suggest, at a later stage in the negotiation, that the other side (rather than you) should contract a third party to arrange transport.

Keeping your ammunition dry

If you pick up something in the other side's position which you can exploit – some statistical mistake, inaccurate information or some flaw in their argument – it's often best not to draw attention to this immediately, but to keep your powder dry for use at a point later in the discussion when it can be used to maximum effect.

Dealing with loaded questions

If you're asked a loaded question in an attempt to weaken your position, there are several options:

● Answer it confidently, briefly, authoritatively – this is the best, most effective and powerful response. Use the minimum number of facts necessary to answer the question

● Ask a question in return – especially useful early on

● Decline to answer it, but link this refusal with something indisputable that has already been discussed

● Question the question. Don't be aggressive, but imply that there's no real value in asking it; in effect, dismissing the question

● Acknowledge it and agree to answer it later, when other matters have been dealt with.

So it's not negotiable?

If the other side say that something is not negotiable, there are three possibilities:

1 It's a ploy

2 They think it is not negotiable, when in fact it is (perhaps a higher authority will give them a new mandate or more flexibility)

3 It really is not negotiable

There are several ways of dealing with this:

- Test it for validity by probing questioning

- Acknowledge it and move on to other points – if you make real progress on these, the other side may be reluctant to throw away the progress made

- Open up other avenues that could be explored if this stumbling block were removed

- Accept it as non-negotiable and ask for something in return

Dealing with threats

Threats are best dealt with by requests for clarification and by probing, challenging questioning. It's important to give the impression that you are not bothered whether or not the threat is carried out – even if you are! If necessary, you can respond along the lines of: "You must do what you must do. It doesn't alter the fact that we ..."

Watch out for the word *but*

Keep a keen look out for the word *but*, as in "We think your proposal is absolutely first-class, but..." In sentences like that, anything before the *but* (sometimes it's a *however* or a *nevertheless*) should be taken with a very large pinch of salt. The sting is in the tail. That's the bit that matters: that's what they are really saying.

Answer it now or later?

When faced with a specific proposal or demand, the question arises: do you respond immediately, or leave it until later? There is no one answer: it depends on the circumstances.

It's often best to respond by questioning and probing the reasoning behind the proposal; then to remain non-committal and inscrutable while you reflect and consider.

Sometimes, however, it's best to strike while the iron is hot – while the other side's words are fresh in your mind. They may have given an indication of their priorities which enables you to identify, and incorporate in your response, something that will help both sides to make progress.

Don't get thrown off balance

Watch out for attempts to:

- Distract your attention so that the other side is in the driving seat and can dominate the discussion

- Change the focus of the discussion so that the end-result benefits the other side

- Introduce red herrings, making you take your eye off the ball

- Complicate the negotiation with unnecessary factors, so that you get bogged down in lots of little details and lose sight of the overall picture

- Cajole you into closing the negotiations before you are 100% satisfied with what's on offer

- Make a counter-offer that seems similar to the original proposal, but is in fact a totally different proposition (for example, changing some of the key elements, such as time or quantity) Make them understand that so far as you are concerned, it's a new proposal. Then make sure you understand thoroughly what's being offered before you decide upon your response

Create the illusion that it doesn't matter

Negotiating strength belongs to the side that is least anxious to reach agreement – so create that illusion. You may be able to introduce the idea that you could get the same result by other means or by going elsewhere, but that you'd prefer to do business with them.

Give them options

Offering the other side the choice of two options can be a good tactic to encourage the other side to move forward.

Floating options you don't want

Try to create scenarios where there is a choice of, say, two or three options. Identify the one you want. Then push gently for one of the other options, with the intention of allowing yourself to be deflected from it onto the one you really want. If you use this tactic, do so cautiously and carefully. Otherwise you might get lumbered with the option you pushed for but don't want!

Dealing with lies and bluff

If you suspect that the other side are bluffing or being economical with the truth, don't call them liars. Make a suggestion that can only be viable if what they're saying is true.

"Sorry, I must have misunderstood..."

Pretending that you have misunderstood something, and asking for clarification, can be a useful tactic. You can take the blame for the misunderstanding, and then either concede or retract the point. You might suggest that you henceforth record points as they are agreed, so that there are no further misunderstandings and both sides know exactly what has been agreed.

This tactic can be used:

● If you suspect the other side of trying to mislead or bamboozle you

● To slow down the negotiations

● To retract something you have conceded without losing face

● To buy time to plan your response or your next move

● To gain a concession

Handling bottlenecks

If the negotiation stalls and you find yourself in a bottleneck, there are several options you can consider:

- Adjourn and chat informally

- Use the break to explore what's really bothering the other side and what they really need

- Find something new to throw into the equation

- Try to get things moving by getting agreement on unimportant points

- Once you have reached agreement on some of the minor stuff, it's more likely that you'll be able to make progress on the big issue(s)

The negotiating environment

Remember that most negotiations take place in an ever-changing environment. Timing is often crucial to the outcome. The position of either side – and the balance of power – could be significantly affected by seasonal variations and slight changes in any of a hundred and one things: for example, share prices, government policy or regulations, the availability of material supplies, exchange rates, etc.

Using an afterthought as a lever

Save one thing you want until later, when everything else has been agreed. Then say something like: "There's just one thing I almost forgot. Can I assume …" You need to minimize the importance of whatever it is you're asking for, but to make the whole deal seem dependent on this one thing. If not used carefully, this tactic could backfire and cause bad feeling or even the loss of the whole negotiation. So use it only if you're sure the circumstances and the mood are right.

Is it ethical?

If you feel uneasy because you have concealed some information that you know would help the other side, consider what a reasonable person would think about this. If you're pretty sure that they would think you should disclose what you know, then do that.

If you have doubts about the propriety or the ethics of the way you're behaving, there is one simple test. Ask yourself whether you would be embarrassed if the details were to be published in a newspaper. Unless you have an amazingly thick skin, that's an almost infallible test.

Dirty tricks can come home to roost. If you get a reputation for lying or for misleading the other side, it won't do you any good in the long run. Ethical behavior is good for business.

15 Summary of dos and don'ts

In this book we have covered a great deal of ground, from key negotiating principles and core skills to the tactics and practicalities of effective negotiation. This chapter provides a handy summary of best practice. You can use it as a last-minute crib sheet, before you go into a negotiation, to remind yourself of things to do and things to avoid.

Dos

Do:

- Take accurate notes (a notepad can be more useful than the most sophisticated piece of IT kit) – note especially key details (if possible verbatim) of the other side's facts, figures, arguments, offers and suggestions

- Listen really carefully to every word the other side say

- Let them know that they have been heard and understood

- Be polite but persistent

- Make it as easy as you can for the other side to change their position

- Search for common ground

- Favor a joint approach to problem-solving: "*How can we solve this in a way that suits both of us?*"

- Keep cool: if things get heated, a question or a little humor may help to diffuse the tension

- Take care with humor: it can be personal and sensitive. Self-deprecating humor and light asides often work best

- Use the power of silence: it can put pressure on the other side to respond to a question or provide more information, and it can be the best way of handling a verbal or personal attack

- Ask for an adjournment if anything totally unexpected or new is put to you

- Move forward slowly – sudden leaps can make the other side nervous and suspicious

- Remember that it's better to lose a battle and win the war: striving to win absolutely every point can lead to stalemate or lose-lose. It's better to give way on small points and keep your main objectives intact

- Build in early benefits to the agreement for both sides if you can: this provides a strong incentive to prevent any backsliding

- Decline to reopen the debate on a point that has already been agreed. Stick to your guns and reassure them of the benefits to them

- Beware of anyone who seems to be extremely nice: be extra alert

- If the other side hesitate or try to back out after you've reached agreement, be gentle. Don't force it though. Sympathize. Point out the potential harm to their reputation if they are regarded as an unreliable negotiator. But do this diplomatically. Tread very carefully

- Be really positive about the benefits to both sides. Enthusiasm is catching

- Use the feel, felt found technique: "*I know how you feel. That's how I used to feel. But what I've found is ...*"

- Make your word your bond: establish a reputation for honesty, commitment and 100% implementation of any agreement you sign up to

- De-brief yourself once the negotiation is over. Ask yourself:

  - How successful was I in achieving my objectives?

  - What factors contributed to success?

  - What went wrong?

  - What could I do better or differently next time?

Don'ts

Don't:

- Blame the other side

- Criticize or antagonize the other side

- Undermine their dignity or let them lose face (for example, by criticizing someone in the presence of their superiors)

- Try to score points off them

- Retaliate

- Say things like: "*I insist on*"

- Lose your temper

- Be too committed to doing a deal

- Have an adjournment without summarizing and recording the discussion so far

- Be afraid to be tough

- Discuss major issues at the end of the day, when you're tired and energy levels are low

- Allow yourself to be brow-beaten into agreeing to something simply because of the clock. If some substantive issue remains to be resolved, insist on adjourning the negotiations and resuming at a later date

- Give the other side an ultimatum, without thinking really carefully about the implications. Look at it from the other side's perspective. Only use it if you're absolutely sure that there are no other options. You'll lose credibility if you withdraw it. It's the last resort

Why not try our other business titles?

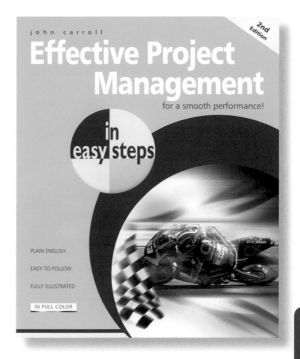

Understanding and working slavishly to set leadership models can mean missing some of the fundamental elements that will make you an effective leader - being true to yourself and others whilst at the same time maximizing your own strengths and personality characteristics. Leadership in easy steps provides a pragmatic and practical look at the key elements that will help you to become a truly effective leader of people.

Leadership in easy steps is designed to help you discover more about you, your personal strengths and your potential and so become a genuinely inspirational leader of people.

As well as describing some of the fundamental elements of leadership, Leadership in easy steps also provides a number of simple exercises and assessment techniques that will help you determine your own unique style of leadership.

This essential project management title will show you how to make sure your project is successful. It focuses on the key skills a manager needs to develop for a smooth running project, and a timely arrival at the finishing line.

It includes examples for most key documents such as the terms of reference, business case and project plan. It addresses team building and good communications. It covers the typical project stages with helpful lists of applicable tasks and deliverables, which effectively provides a blueprint for planning an entire project.

If you're a first time project manager, let this book take you through the essential project stages in easy steps, and take note of the applicable tasks and deliverables.

If you're an experienced project manager, this book provides a valuable source of inspiration for making projects run smoothly and satisfactorily. Covering risk-management together with insights on how to plan, lead, organize and control a project - simply a fountain of knowledge!

Available to buy online at www.ineasysteps.com

Update and improve your skills

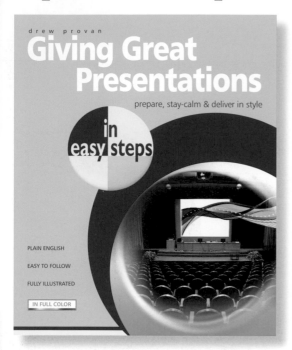

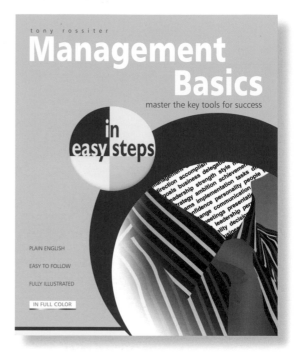

When was the last time you attended a presentation and thought "That was fantastic! I really enjoyed listening to the speaker and learned something today..."? It doesn't happen often enough, because most people who present give mediocre talks at best. But it shouldn't be like this.

Presenting information or data, whether it be one on one to your boss, or at an international conference to an audience of thousands, is very much part of modern business and academic life. But such occasions are feared by most people, and even people who are outwardly confident in their work can fall apart at the podium and give the most mediocre presentations simply through anxiety, nervousness and lack of preparation.

With patience and practice and using the guidance in Giving Great Presentations in easy steps you will soon be giving memorable presentations and become a real asset to your organization! Or if you're just planning to talk to a small group of enthusiasts at a local club this book will help you there, too!

Also available as an ebook

Whether you are an experienced manager or about to take up your first management job, Management Basics in easy steps will be of real help to you in the workplace. It is a lively, easy-to-read book and full of practical information and common sense advice on Management fundamentals. Management consultant, Tony Rossiter's clear, humorous writing style and comprehensive content make Management Basics in easy steps a compelling read.

His management tips and advice will show you:

- How to manage people: your staff, your colleagues, your customers and even your boss

- How to organize yourself and make the most effective use of your time

- How to focus on the vital 20% of your work that accounts for most of the results

and much, much more!

Comes with useful worksheets - a complete guide for easy reference.

Also available as an ebook

Available to buy online at www.ineasysteps.com

Grow your business

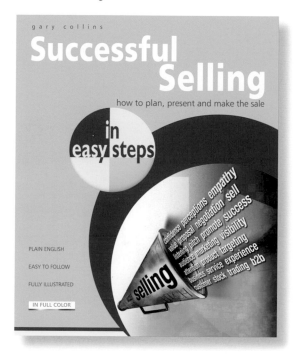

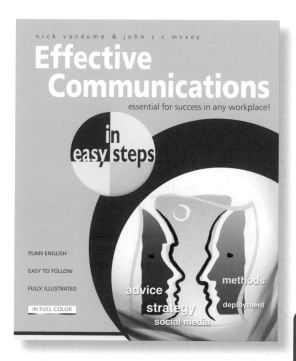

Successful Selling in easy steps is written both for the individual, self-employed sales rep as well as for use by large corporations as a great sales 'tool' for their staff. The author, Gary Collins, has been in sales management for global blue-chip companies for over 24 years and has amassed some inspirational knowledge that he passes on to you here.

Successful Selling in easy steps is packed with great tips and advice on selling. It will help you to:

- Have a positive and competitive attitude to ensure that you achieve all of the goals that you set yourself or are set for you

- Develop outstanding communications skills

- Learn how to gain valuable information with great questioning techniques

- Plan your time, customers and sales calls to optimize your efficiency and effectiveness

- Close your sales presentations early to maximize your productivity

We all communicate, every day, all of the time. So why can communications go so wrong in the workplace? Sometimes it is because the wrong methods are used at the wrong times, and sometimes it is because the communications process becomes too complicated and bogged down in corporate jargon.

Effective Communications in easy steps will show you how to:

- Create a practical Communications Strategy that works

- Understand how, and why, to evaluate your strategy

- Build and maintain websites that keep delivering

- Unravel the mysteries of social media

- Explode the myths about communications at work

- Get your message across using the right channel to engage your audience.

Also available as an ebook

Available to buy online at www.ineasysteps.com

Boost your creativity

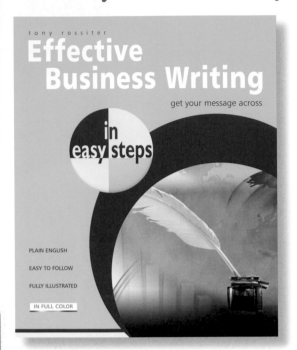

The ability to communicate effectively in writing is a key business skill. Whether you're drafting a lengthy company report or sending a short email to colleagues, it's vital to get it right. That means being clear and concise, and writing in a style that's acceptable to the reader. If your writing is difficult to understand or written in an inappropriate style, it won't be effective.

Effective Business Writing in easy steps is the ideal guide for anyone who needs guidance with writing in the workplace. Its clear, concise, easy-to-read style means that you'll soon master the fundamental skills to communicate effectively in business. It covers the basic tools such as plain English, vocabulary, spelling, punctuation and grammar, to preparing and checking your presentation, then how to put it into practice when writing documents such as letters, emails, notes, reports and speeches and many more.

Whether you are already in a marketing job, aspire to having one or want to grow your business, Effective Marketing in easy steps will help you to become a successful marketer.

By keeping it simple, Catriona MacKay has combined her own business experience with established best practice to give you a practical guide to marketing.

Her great marketing tips and advice will help you:

- Write a successful marketing plan

- Avoid making costly mistakes

- Encourage good marketing practice at work

- Use what you know to make your business grow

- Devise effective marketing for today's market including how to use online resources

Essential for those who want to grasp the key marketing skills without getting bogged down in academic theories. Includes worksheets to get you started.

Available to buy online at www.ineasysteps.com

D

E

F

U

V

W